W9-BYR-313

ellen gormley

one skein
crochet

de-stash beautifully, one skein at a time

Interweave

dedication

For my kids, Maura and Patrick—the reason I do everything I do. And for Tom, who gives me free rein to be myself.

fwcommunity.com

Interweave®

interweave.com

23 22 21 20 19 5 4 3 2 1

SRN: 19CR01

ISBN-13: 978-1-63250-668-9

Editorial Director: Kerry Bogert

Editor: Nathalie Mornu

Technical Editor: Tian Connaughton

Art Director and Cover Designer: Ashlee Wadeson

Interior Layout: Alex Doherty

Illustrators: Tian Connaughton and Ann Swanson

Photography

    Finished samples: Harper Point Photography

    All other photos: George Boe

Stylist: Tina Gill

Hair and Makeup: Valerie Salls

contents

introduction

I have lonely skeins, and you probably do, too! There's no need to feel guilty about it. I have a strategy for solving this, and those lonesome hanks will blossom with their singular potential.

Like many crocheters, I'm often drawn to luscious multicolored sock yarns, super chunky solids, and soft wools. The colors are amazing, and they look so fantastic on the hank. But as I admire the yarn in the store, I wonder, "What to do with it? How much should I buy when I don't have a specific project in mind?" So, unable to resist, I buy just one skein. And now I have one single, gorgeous skein and no plan. The poor thing sits like a velveteen rabbit in my stash bin, unrecognized for its amazing possibilities!

Do you recognize yourself in this story, too? Your particulars might be slightly different. Maybe you have one skein left over from an epic project, but no receipt to take it back to the store. Or perhaps a non-stitcher gave you one ball as a thoughtful gift, with no clue that having only one is very limiting. You don't know what to do with these singles. They're too good to give away. But what project can you make with just one skein?!

Well, I have a plan—lots of plans, in fact! To begin with, I have a number of methods for squeezing out every last yard and maximizing just one skein into a completed project—for example, integrating the edging while stitching, working two pieces at the same time

(I call this the Dynamic Duo strategy), and Divide and Conquer (which means splitting the ball evenly in two). This book teaches you ten strategies, and a few of them can even be applied to larger hanks so that you can happily stitch in pattern until the yarn runs out! Crocheting a rectangle until all the yarn is used is a viable plan, but the strategies in this book help you make something creative and functional that is also beautiful and an efficient use of yarn. Every project in this book is specially designed to push the limit of one skein so that there's little to no yarn left over. The Bruges Wedge Cowl, the Corner Garden Shawlette, and the Tumbling Motifs Scarf are all projects that can easily turn into bigger projects if you have more yarn.

All 15 projects let you use up one entire skein of yarn and not waste it. No more lonely skeins! No more orphan hanks! And not only that—with just one skein, your project can probably be made in just a few days or less. You'll make great headway blowing through your stash in short order—gifts galore!

And if you feel inspired to design your own one-skein masterpiece, this book contains tips to help you stitch your vision into reality. So go stash diving (or shop with freedom and happiness) and see what you can make today. Then post your finished projects on Instagram with the hashtag **#oneskeincrochet.**

chapter 1
getting started

This book is different from other one-skein books because all the projects were designed to maximize full balls of yarn without waste. It's not a competition to create multiple tiny projects using the least amount of yarn. Instead the projects show you how to make the most exciting, interesting, and substantial projects possible from just one ball. So if you've got a stash of lone skeins (and what yarn junkie doesn't?) this is your opportunity to make a significant dent in it—and no more leftovers!

HOW TO USE THIS BOOK

To use yarns efficiently with beautiful results, you can approach this book in two ways. Either follow the instructions for the fifteen projects as specified and blissfully stitch along, or throw caution to the wind and design your own patterns using the ten strategies I describe for maximizing yarn.

You can even do both, taking advantage of the book to the fullest by combining both approaches. For example, you might take the shape and strategy of the Coral Reef Scarf but add your own favorite stitch pattern and use a different edging to create something completely new and original.

Choosing a Pattern

The 15 projects in this book fully use a single skein of yarn. Some are perfect for small amounts of yarn and some for larger. If you happen to have one of the yarns used in this book, jackpot! You can now complete one project with a single skein. If you want to buy a skein to make one of the projects, know that just one will yield a complete project. So affordable! You might splurge a little on luxury yarn, since you'll know your total cost right from the start!

To use yarn from your stash, determine how much yardage you've got, as well as its yarn weight—not the weight of the ball. (If the label is missing and you need help figuring out how much there is, see Measuring Yardage on Unlabeled Skeins. To determine the yarn weight, compare your yarn to **figure 1**.) Once you know your yardage and yarn weight, look at the table called Project Yardage and Weights, at far right, to see which project is most similar in length and

weight to your yarn. (They're listed from shortest to longest.) That's the project you should make. Just make sure you have the same yardage—or a little more—and the same weight as the yarn specified in the pattern.

If your stash yarn is a different weight than the specified project yarn, but you think it would still look great in the project you want to make, if it has the right drape, and if you have a reasonable amount of yardage, give it a try anyway.

Understanding Yardage

Every ball, hank, or skein comes in a different yardage. There's no standard for an amount of yardage for yarn across brands. Because of that, you can't assume that a ball of Brand A has the same number of yards (meters) as a ball of Brand B. You can't substitute by the weight of the skein, either. For example, if a skein of Brand A yarn weighs 1.75 oz (50 g) and Brand B weighs 1.75 oz (50 g), they don't necessarily have the same yardage because they may be different yarn weights. (That's not the same as ball weight. I know this is confusing—see Weighty Matters, below.) It's like people—two people with a height difference of one foot (30.5 cm) can both weigh 175 pounds (79.3 kg). Similarly, a ball of chunky weight yarn can weigh 3 oz (85 g) but measure only 175 yards (160 m), while a ball of worsted weight yarn that also weighs 3 oz (85 g) comes on a skein containing 315 yards (288 m). The balls weigh the same because the yarns are different weights—one is thicker than the other.

Weighty Matters

On the yarn's label, the weight of the ball will be listed. That gives the ball's weight on a scale. The word "weight" is also used to describe the thickness of one strand of yarn, as shown in **figure 1.** Weights range from really fat yarns like bulky and super bulky down to the finest yarns, which are called sock or fingering.

Measuring Yardage on Unlabeled Skeins

You grab a ball of yarn from your stash bin only to find that its label has mysteriously disappeared. Or you only have part of a skein left over from another project. How do you know how many yards you have to work with? Here are several ways to measure the yarn. The first method is the only precise one; all the others merely give you an estimate. And don't hold the yarn under much tension as you measure it—stretching it will yield an imprecise number.

Measure it with a yardstick. Place a yardstick flat on a table, unwind the yarn, and pull it one yard at a time across the yardstick, as if you were measuring fabric at a craft store. As you do so, count the lengths.

Have someone else ball up the measured yarn at the edge of the table so the yarn doesn't tangle. This is the most accurate but also the most tedious method, and it's easy to lose count.

Yarn weight 1 | Super fine, Sock, Baby, Fingering

Yarn weight 2 | Fine, Sportweight

Yarn weight 3 | Light, DK, Light worsted

Yarn weight 4 | Medium, Worsted

Yarn weight 5 | Bulky, Chunky

Yarn weight 6 | Super bulky

Figure 1: Yarn weights.

PROJECT YARDAGE AND WEIGHTS	
Oval and Out Scarf	112 yards (102 m), super bulky 6
Narrow as Necessary Scarf	136 yards (125 m), sportweight 2
Tumbling Motifs Scarf	150 yards (137 m), DK 3
Pentagon Mitts	166 yards (152 m), sock weight 1
Handled Purse	170 yards (156 m), worsted 4
Greenery Hat	186 yards (170 m), worsted 4
Star Stitch Hat	197 yards (180 m), worsted 4
Horizontal Slouch Hat	218 yards (200 m), worsted 4
Coral Reef Scarf	220 yards (200 m), worsted 4
Bruges Wedge Cowl	250 yards (228 m), DK 3
Bruges Motif Top	255 yard (233 m), DK 3
Corner Garden Shawlette	275 yards (251 m), DK 3
Solomon's Wrap	306 yards (280 m), DK 3
Market Bag	432 yards (395 m), DK 3
One Motif Baby Blanket	867 yards (792 m), worsted 4

Figure 2

Figure 3

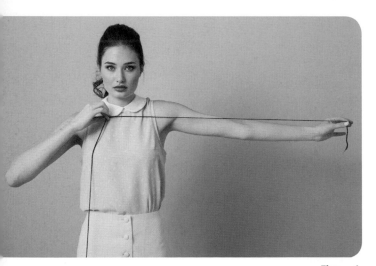

Figure 4

Measure it with your reach. First, a little background: I know that if I hold yarn in my left hand and extend my arm, pulling the yarn across my chest to my right collarbone, that span measures 1 yard. I have really long arms, however, so what I'm describing may not apply to your own body. So find your measurement: Use a measuring tape to measure your reach and determine where the 1-yard (or 1-meter) spot is for you **(figure 2)**. Then you won't need a yardstick but will have a fairly accurate measurement as you pull the yarn and count the number of times you can span the reach, as follows.

1. Holding the end of the yarn loosely in your non-dominant hand, place both hands at the 1-yard (1-meter) spot along your collarbone. Then firmly grasp the end of the yarn with your dominant hand **(figure 3)**.

2. Straighten your dominant arm, pulling the yarn with it **(figure 4)**. That counts as 1 yard (1 meter). Drop the yarn in your dominant hand, bring that hand back to the yarn being held loosely by your nondominant hand, and again grasp the yarn with your dominant hand.

3. Repeat step 2, counting each yard (meter) until you've measured all the yarn. Again, it's helpful to have someone else balling up the measured yarn as you work so it doesn't get tangled.

Measure by weight. You'll need a kitchen scale. Start by unwinding exactly 5 yards (or 5 meters, if you work in the metric system) of your yarn and placing it on the scale—but don't cut it. Note how much that weighs in grams. Then place the entire ball of yarn on the scale (including the first 5 yards or meters) and take note of the total weight, again in grams. Now it's time to do some math:

1. Divide the 5-yard (5-meter) weight by 5. Now you know what 1 yard (1 meter) weighs.

2. Divide the total weight of the ball by the weight of 1 yard (1 meter). The result is the total yardage.

For example, let's say that your 5 yards (5 m) of yarn weighs 3 grams, and that the entire ball weighs 300 grams.

3 grams ÷ 5 = 0.6 grams.

So 1 yard (1 m) weighs 0.6 grams.

300 ÷ 0.6 = 500.

The ball has approximately 500 yards (500 m) in it.

Measure with a commercial yarn meter. Be aware, however, that according to rumors, they're not accurate all the time.

Measure with a yarn swift. If you have a yarn swift, expand it and use a flexible measuring tape to measure the circumference of the swift at the waist (the narrower middle section), where the yarn will rest. (Remember that the wider the swift is open, the larger the circumference, and the more closed, the smaller the circumference. Don't assume that every time you use the swift it's opened to the same exact circumference. Measure the circumference each time you're calculating yardage.) Once you know the circumference of the swift, wind the yarn around it, counting each lap. Afterward, multiply the number of

An inexpensive kitchen scale capable of weighing small amounts in grams can help you determine yardage.

laps times the circumference to get the total yardage of yarn. Then re-ball the yarn.

There's a second option for using a swift to measure. If the yarn is already in a hank, you can do the following:

1. Untwist it and put it on the yarn swift, then extend the swift as far as the hank will allow (**figure 5**).

2. Measure the circumference of the open swift (**figure 6**).

3. Count the number of strands in the hank (**figure 7**).

4. Multiply the number of strands by the circumference of the swift to get the total yardage of the yarn.

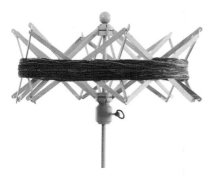

Figure 5

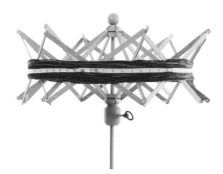

Figure 6

Figure 7

Gauge Is Critical

Gauge is the number of stitches per row or round, both in length and height. A pattern typically presents this information in terms of how many stitches are in 4 inches (10 cm). It may read: 12 sts and 12 rows = 4" (10 cm). This means that in the given stitch pattern, if you place a hard ruler against your project, anywhere you measure you should be able to count 12 sts across 4 inches (10 cm) and 12 rows in a height of 4 inches (10 cm). If you're getting too many stitches per inch, you need to increase your hook size to create larger stitches. If you're getting too few stitches per inch, decrease your hook size to create smaller stitches.

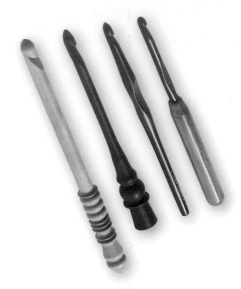

Because every yard matters with these projects, you must keep an eye on your gauge. A gauge swatch is always a great idea. Yardage spent on making a separate gauge swatch is not factored into the total amount of yarn needed for each project, however. Because of this, you'll need to follow the project instructions and after a few inches, stop and measure. Do not cut the yarn but determine if your gauge is matching the project instructions. If necessary, you may need to pull out the initial stitches and begin again with a different hook to achieve the correct gauge. These projects were designed to have very little yarn left over. If you happen to run out of yarn before you finish the project, your stitches are too big and you may need to rip out one or two rows/rounds and crochet a little more tightly to successfully finish.

If you have yarn left over, many of the projects allow you to keep going extra rounds or rows until all the yarn is used. The Bruges Wedge Cowl, the Oval and Out Scarf, the One Motif Baby Blanket, the Tumbling Motifs Scarf, the Coral Reef Scarf, and the Corner Garden Shawlette are all excellent for continuing on if your skein has more yardage than specified in the pattern. So, on those projects, if you get to the end of the pattern and you still have more yarn left over and want to use it up, just keep going in the established pattern. For all the other projects not listed above, consider using leftover yarn to create a border, or add tassels or fringe.

Predicting Whether You Have Enough Yarn Left

If you run out of yarn mid-row, round, or motif, you'll be forced to rip out a bit to get to the previously completed row, round, or motif. Let's be honest—with a one-skein project, this is not a tragedy. Nonetheless, here are different methods for anticipating if you'll run out of yarn in a given row, round, or motif, and all it takes is some simple arithmetic.

Method 1: Calculate yardage by the stitch

You'll need a barrette or clip and a tape measure.

1. Make some stitches in the intended stitch pattern.

2. Clip a barrette after the last stitch made to mark that spot.

3. Unravel one stitch or repeat of the pattern. Add 1" (2.5 cm). The distance between the barrette and the added inch is the amount of yarn needed to make one stitch or repeat.

4. Determine how many stitches you need to make, and multiply that number by the yardage per stitch. That's how much yarn you still need.

For example, say you're making a project in seed stitch and it takes 1½" (3.8 cm) of yarn to make 1 stitch.

Now let's imagine that you're almost finished crocheting the project but still need to make 5 stitches in a partially finished row you're on, and then you have eight more rows left with 12 stitches in each. First, calculate how many stitches you still need to make.

5 for this row + [8 rows × 12 stitches] = 101 stitches over the nine remaining rows to finish the pattern as written.

Next, calculate the amount of yarn needed.

Imperial: 101 stitches × 1½" per stitch = 151½"

Metric: 101 stitches × 3.8 cm per stitch = 384 cm.

It requires 151½" (384 cm)—nearly 4¼ yards (almost 4 m)—to finish the project.

Narrow as Necessary Scarf

Method 2: Calculate yardage by the row/round

You'll need two flexible barrettes, bulldog clips, or some other method of marking the yarn, as well as a tape measure.

1. As you're nearing the end of the yarn ball, clip a flexible hair barrette after the last stitch at the end of the row or round.

2. Rip out the last row or round and place another flexible barrette after the end of what is now the last row or round.

3. Measure the amount of yarn between the barrettes. This tells you how much yarn was needed to crochet the row or round.

4. Measure the yarn that remains. Subtract 3" (7.5 cm) from it. (This 3" [7.5 cm] distance is the amount of tail that's ideal to have when fastening off and weaving in.)

5. To figure out how many rows' or rounds' worth of yarn you still have, divide the remaining yarn by the amount needed to crochet a row or round.

Here's an example:

After ripping out your last row and measuring between the barrettes, you find that one row requires 12 yards (11 m) of yarn.

You measure the remaining yarn, and you have 53 yards (48.5 m) left.

To calculate how many rows you can make, divide the remaining yardage by the yardage needed per row:

Imperial: 53 yards (amount remaining) ÷ 12 yards (needed per row) = 4.4 rows

Metric: 48.5 m (amount remaining) ÷ 11 (needed per row) = 4.4 rows

You can work only 4.4 more rows, which is only four complete rows, and that still leaves you plenty for the tail.

This works only if the rest of the rows are going to be the same length as the one you measured. If you're increasing in rounds or on a growing triangle, the amount of yarn needed per row or round will continually increase. If you're working a triangle and know that you're only increasing by 1 stitch every row, you can calculate by the stitch (see Method 1) to get a rough estimate.

Star Stitch Hat

DESIGNING YOUR OWN ONE-SKEIN PROJECTS

In this book, DIY means "design it yourself"! Never be limited by single skeins again. With the strategies in this book, you'll be able to see potential in every ball. By describing how I applied the strategies to the projects in this book, I'll show you how to apply the same strategies to your own stash. When you design your own project, you have the joy of making many decisions that, combined, will create a completely unique item. It will be yours and represent your likes and preferences.

Choosing the Right Skein for a Project

Combining the perfect yarn with the ideal project in the right stitch pattern is the recipe for success. As you reach for a skein to consider, there are many things to think about. You may first be attracted to its color, but texture, weight, fiber content, and yardage all matter when deciding what project the yarn could turn into.

Texture. The yarn may be flat or round, nubby or fluffy, smooth or with a halo—all of these factors will completely change the appearance of a project. If the yarn has a great deal of texture, you may not be able to see an intricate stitch pattern. If the yarn is smooth, it won't have the same ethereal quality that a wispy or haloed yarn might have. A fuzzy or nubby yarn may look great for a blanket or pillow, but you might not want to make it into a top because it will visually add bulk to your frame. (Or maybe you would! It's totally up to you!)

Weight. The weight or thickness of the yarn makes a difference in the finished project. A very thin or fine yarn will make much smaller stitches than a bulkier yarn. Imagine a finished project like a shawl made in a thin sock-weight yarn and also made from a bulky-weight yarn. Which one appeals to you more? If your goal is to make a shawl, then choosing the weight you want will matter.

Fiber. How do you know if you're choosing the right fiber for a project? In general, natural animal fibers are warmer than plant fibers. If you're designing a hat meant to be worn when playing in the snow, a wool or alpaca or a blend of those would probably be more suitable than cotton or bamboo. Conversely, if you live in a warm climate and want a delicate wrap to wear to an afternoon wedding, a warm animal fiber may not appeal to you. You might want a cotton or rayon or linen blend instead. Choose the fiber based on how and where the project will be used.

Yardage. The larger the project, the more yardage will be needed. No matter how lacy you make a project, one ball that only has 150 yards (137.1 m) in it will never be big enough to make a throw blanket. However, 150 yards (137.1 m) might make a great headband or lacy hat. The yardage has to be respected, no matter what. It's nonnegotiable.

Selecting a Stitch

You can choose your favorite stitches, of course, but some of the stitches that get the most mileage from a skein include the ones on these two pages.

Key

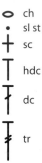

- ○ ch
- • sl st
- † sc
- T hdc
- T dc
- ‡ tr

Treble Mesh

Ch an odd number + 5 chs. (For example, 23 + 5 = ch 28.)

Row 1: Tr in the 6th ch from hook (skipped chains count as first tr + ch-1 sp), *ch 1, sk 1 ch, tr in next ch; rep from * across.

Row 2: Ch 5 (counts as first tr + ch 1), turn, *sk 1 ch, tr in next tr; rep from * across.

Rows 3-7: Rep Row 2.

Repeat this sequence for as long as desired, then fasten off.

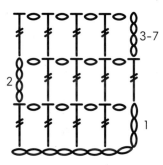

Stitch diagram for Treble Mesh.

Bruges Lace

Ch 9.

Row 1: (RS) Dc in 6th ch from hook and in each of last 3 chs. (4 dc, 1 ch-5 sp).

Row 2: Ch 5, turn, dc in each dc across.

Rows 3-5: Rep Row 2.

Row 6: Ch 1, turn, sc in first 2 sts, hdc in next st, dc in last st.

Row 7: Ch 5, turn, dc in first st, hdc in next st, sc in last 2 sts.

Rows 8-15: Rep Rows 6 and 7.

Row 16: Rep Row 6.

Row 17: Ch 5, turn, dc in each dc across.

Row 18: Ch 2, sl st in ch-5 sp of Row 4, ch 2, turn, dc in each of next 4 dc.

Row 19: Ch 5, turn, dc in each of next 4 dc.

Row 20: Ch 2, sl st in ch-5 sp of Row 2, ch 2, turn, dc in each of next 4 dc.

Row 21: Ch 5, turn, dc in each of next 4 dc.

Repeat this sequence for as long as desired, then fasten off.

Stitch diagram for Bruges Lace.

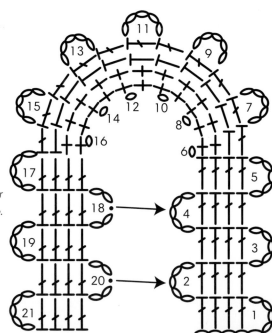

Lacy Fans

Ch a multiple of 8 + 4 chs. (For example, 32 + 4 = ch 36.)

Row 1: Sc in 6th ch from hook (5 skipped chs count as first dc, 1 ch, 1 sk ch), *ch 3, sk 3 chs, sc in next ch; rep from * across to last 2 chs, ch 1, sk next ch, dc in last ch.

Row 2: Ch 1, turn, sc in first dc, *ch 1, ([dc, ch 1] 3 times, dc) in next ch-3 sp, ch 1, sc in next ch-3 sp; rep from * across to last ch-1 sp, ch 1, sk last ch-1 sp, sc in last dc.

Row 3: Ch 4 (counts as first dc + ch 1), turn, sk next ch-1 sp, sc in next ch-1 sp, ch 3, sk next ch-1 sp, sc in next ch-1 sp, *ch 3, sk next (ch-1 sp, sc, ch-1 sp), sc in next ch-1 sp, ch 3, sk next ch-1 sp, sc in next ch-1 sp; rep from * across to last ch-1 sp, ch 1, sk last ch-1 sp, dc in last sc.

Rows 4-15: Rep Rows 2 and 3.

Repeat this sequence for as long as desired, then fasten off.

V-Stitch

Ch a multiple of 2 + 2 chs. (For example, 24 + 2 = ch 26.)

Row 1: 2 dc in 4th ch from hook, *sk next ch, 2 dc in next ch; rep from * to last 2 ch, sk next ch, dc in last ch.

Row 2: Ch 3 (count as a dc), turn, *sk next 2 sts, 2 dc between 2 dc; rep from * to last 2 sts, sk 1 dc, dc in last dc.

Rows 3-10: Rep Row 2.

Repeat this sequence for as long as desired, then fasten off.

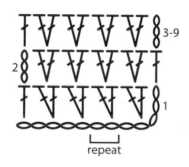

Stitch diagram for V-stitch.

Ropes & Ladders

Ch a multiple of 4 + 2 chs. (For example, 16 + 2 = ch 18.)

Row 1: Sc in 2nd ch from hook, *ch 3, sk 3 chs, sc in next ch; rep from * across.

Row 2: Ch 1, sc in first st, *ch 3, sk 3 chs, sc in next sc; rep from * across.

Rows 3-20: Rep Row 2.

Repeat this sequence for as long as desired, then fasten off.

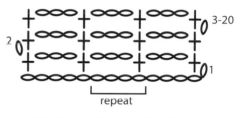

Stitch diagram for Ropes & Ladders.

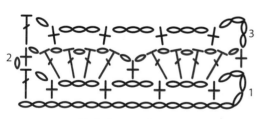

Stitch diagram for Lacy Fans.

Calculating How Much Yarn You'll Need

The designing spirit is often one of flexibility and spontaneity. My favorite approach is just to try it and see. Just start your idea; it's not a major commitment to see how big a project can become using one skein. Worst case scenario: you're out one skein's worth of time, but likely you'll have gained valuable information about how to do things differently. Just undo all your stitching and try again. Maybe in your next swatch you'd use a different stitch pattern, a different edging, add more or fewer chains, or adjust the shape. Time spent learning is never time wasted.

Still, if you find it hard to go with the flow and see what happens, you can make some educated guesses about how much yarn you'll need by referring to the standard yardage requirements given in the charts here. These provide a rough estimate of yarn amounts needed to complete basic projects. You can use your calculations and check them against the charts to see if you're in the ballpark. Or skip the calculations altogether and use the charts as a general starting point.

For things other than scarves, hats, and cowls, you can search "one-skein" on popular pattern sites to see how much yardage is needed to accomplish projects. That might inspire you and give you a visual clue of the size it's possible to make from one skein.

Also, search the specific yarn you plan to use on popular pattern sites and see what projects have been made from it. You can check how many balls are needed to complete the project, and this will give you a visual clue what's possible with one skein. For example, if a women's small sleeveless vest uses two balls of yarn then, using a similar stitch pattern, you could probably make something the size of either the front or the back of the vest using one ball.

If you would like to widen your search for options, look at projects on websites that require only two balls of a specific yarn. You can guess what the item might look like if it were half the size, using only one ball of the same yarn. Working your brain in this way is great practice for visualizing the possibilities when evaluating a lone skein.

Or you could try this unscientific method: Hold the skein or ball of yarn in your hands. Close your eyes … think of what kind of project this could become. What kind of project, when squished in your hands, is approximately the same size as the ball of yarn? Can you imagine squishing a scarf into that same area? A baby blanket? A cowl? A hat?

Finally, you can calculate how much yardage you need per row, or by area, by making a swatch. This is a more complicated process than just glancing at the charts here, but it's far more precise. The swatch points you in the right direction.

How to calculate yardage per row:

1. Before you start making the project, crochet a swatch without cutting the yarn. Measure it and count how many rows it contains; also measure the height of a row. (Alternately, you can divide the length of the swatch by the number of rows to determine the height of each row.)

2. Mark where the yarn comes out of the swatch by putting a barrette or a bulldog clip on that spot, then unravel the swatch. Measure how many yards (m) were used to make the swatch.

3. Divide the yardage by the number of rows or rounds so that you now know how many yards were needed to complete one row or round.

FOR A SCARF

The chart below offers some guidelines if you were to make a scarf that is 6 × 40". If you would like to make a scarf that is a different size, you will estimate the yardage accordingly. To make a scarf half the proposed size, you will need half the yarn. To make the scarf 50 percent larger, you will need 50 percent more yarn, etc.

Number of sts / inch	Amount needed
2	180 yds (165 m)
3	240 yds (219 m)
4	320 yds (293 m)
5	360 yds (329 m)
6	480 yds (439 m)

Tumbling Motifs Scarf

FOR A COWL

Remember, a cowl is just a scarf that is joined on the ends to create a tube. This might help you visualize how much space and yarn is needed to create your project. To make a cowl that is wider, we use an example that is 6 × 20" (15 × 51 cm) but we want the cowl to be 9" (23 cm) — that is, 50 percent wider than the original 6" [15 cm]) — so we need to add 50 percent more yarn. If the 6 × 20" (15 × 51 cm) cowl for 4 stitches per inch (most likely a medium-weight yarn) uses 160 yards (146.3 m), 50 percent of 160 yards is 80 yards, so add the 80 yards to 160 yards, and the new total for a wider cowl that measures 9 × 20" (23 × 51 cm) is 240 yards (219.4 m).

Number of sts / inch	6 × 20" (15 × 51 cm)	6 × 30" (15 × 76 cm)	6 × 40" (15 × 101.5 cm)	6 × 50" (15 × 127 cm)
2	180 yds (165 m)	140 yds (128 m)	180 yds (165 m)	240 yds (219 m)
3	240 yds (219 m)	180 yds (165 m)	240 yds (219 m)	320 yds (293 m)
4	320 yds (293 m)	240 yds (219 m)	320 yds (293 m)	450 yds (411 m)
5	360 yds (329 m)	300 yds (274 m)	400 yds (366 m)	
6	480 yds (439 m)	380 yds (347 m)		

FOR HATS

These yardages are for hats with a height of 7" (18 cm).

Number of sts / inch	18" (45.5 cm)	20" (51 cm)	22" (56 cm)
2	100 yds (91 m)	100 yds (91 m)	140 yds (128 m)
3	120 yds (110 m)	120 yds (110 m)	180 yds (165 m)
4	160 yds (146 m)	160 yds (146 m)	240 yds (219 m)
5	180 yds (165 m)	180 yds (165 m)	280 yds (256 m)
6	230 yds (210 m)	230 yds (210 m)	360 yds (329 m)

Here's an example of the math. Refer to **figure 8** as you follow along.

After unraveling and measuring the yarn, you found that it took 80 yards (73.2 m) to make your swatch, which contained six rows.

Imperial: 4" ÷ 6 rows = 0.67"

Metric: 10 cm ÷ 6 rows = 1.7 cm

Each row is 0.67" (1.7 cm) tall.

Imperial: 80 yards ÷ 6 rows = 13.33

Metric: 73.2 m ÷ 6 rows = 12.2 m

Each row requires 13.3 yards (12.2 m) of yarn.

Now that you know how tall each row is and many yards (meters) you need to crochet each row, you can calculate how much yarn you'll need to crochet a longer amount that's the same width.

For instance—continuing with this swatch, and referring to **figure 9**—if it takes 13.3 yards (12.2 m) to make one row 4" (10 cm) wide and 0.67" (1.7 cm) tall, how much yarn will you need to crochet a piece 4 × 12 inches (10 x 30.5 cm)? (Remember word problems in school? And you didn't think you'd find real-life applications for them!)

First, figure out how many rows you'll need to make by dividing the desired length by the length of one row; round that number up or down.

Imperial: 12" ÷ 0.67" = 17.9

Metric: 30.5 cm ÷ 1.7 cm = 17.9

You'll need to crochet 18 rows.

Knowing that, you can calculate how much yarn you'll need by multiplying the number of rows by the yardage needed per row, then round up.

In the case of the example:

Imperial: 18 rows × 13.33 yds needed per row = 239.4 yds

Metric: 18 rows × 12.2 m needed per row = 219.6m

For this example, you would need 240 yards (220 m) to make a piece 4 × 12 inches (10 × 30.5 cm).

How to calculate yardage by area:

First, measure the height and width of the swatch. Mark where the yarn comes out of it, then unravel the swatch. Measure how many yards (m) were used to make the swatch.

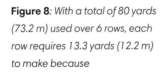 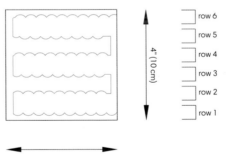

Figure 8: *With a total of 80 yards (73.2 m) used over 6 rows, each row requires 13.3 yards (12.2 m) to make because*

Imperial: *80 yards ÷ 6 rows = 13.3 yards*

Metric: *73.2 m ÷ 6 rows = 12.2 m*

row 6
row 5
row 4
row 3
row 2
row 1

4" (10 cm)

Each row measures 0.67" (1.7 cm) tall because

Imperial: *4" ÷ 6 rows = 0.67"*

Metric: *10 cm ÷ 6 rows = 1.7 cm*

4" (10 cm)

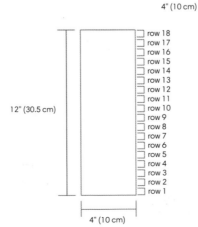

12" (30.5 cm)

row 18
row 17
row 16
row 15
row 14
row 13
row 12
row 11
row 10
row 9
row 8
row 7
row 6
row 5
row 4
row 3
row 2
row 1

4" (10 cm)

Figure 9: *For this example, you start by knowing that each row measures 0.67 inches (1.7 cm) in height and requires 13.3 yards (12.2 m) to crochet.*

To make a strip of fabric 12 inches (30.5 cm) long, you'll need to crochet 18 rows, because

Imperial: *12 inches ÷ 0.67 inches = 17.9 (round up to 18)*

Metric: *30.5 cm ÷ 1.7 cm = 17.9 (round up to 18)*

1. Calculate the area of the swatch by multiplying height by width.

2. Divide the yardage used to make the swatch by the area. This tells you how many yards are required per square inch (or how many meters are required per square centimeter).

For example, let's say your swatch measures 5 × 5" (12.7 × 12.7 cm) and used 30 yards (27.4 m), as shown in **figure 10.**

Imperial: 5 × 5 = 25

Metric: 12.7 × 12.7 = 161

The area is 25 sq. inches (161 sq. cm).

Imperial: 30 yards ÷ 25 sq. inches = 1.2 yards per sq. inch

Metric: 27.4 m ÷ 161 sq. cm = 0.17 m per sq. cm

You need 1.2 yards per sq. inch (0.17 m per sq. cm).

Next, knowing the yards per sq. inch (m per sq. cm), you can calculate how much you'll need for a larger area, as follows.

1. Decide the desired size of the finished item and calculate its area.

2. Multiply the area by the yards required per sq. inch (m required per sq. cm) to find how many yards (meters) you'll need, then round up.

Let's see that in practice. For this example, we'll continue to work with the imaginary swatch in figure 10 that yielded a result of 1.2 yards per sq. inch (0.17 m per sq. cm).

Let's say you want a finished scarf that measures 10 × 30" (25.5 × 76 cm), as shown in **figure 11**. How much yarn will you need?

Imperial: 10" × 30" = 300 sq. inches

Metric: 25.5 cm × 76 cm = 1,938 sq. cm

The area of the desired scarf totals 300 sq. inches (1,938 sq. cm).

Imperial: 300 sq. inches × 1.2 yards needed per sq. inch = 360 yards

Metric: 1,938 sq. cm × 0.17 m needed per sq. cm = 329.5 m

You'll need 360 yards (329.5 m) to make a piece that measures 10 × 30" (25.5 × 76 cm). If your skein is only 200 yards (183 m) long, you can infer without calculating that you can only crochet a piece about half that length, or a little more than 15" (38 cm).

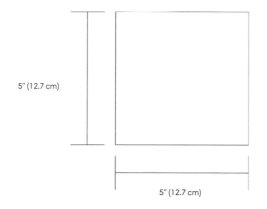

5" (12.7 cm)

5" (12.7 cm)

Figure 10: *In this example, the area is 25 sq. inches (161 sq. cm).*

The swatch required 30 yards (27.4 m) to make. To calculate yards required to make each sq. inch (m per sq. cm), divide the amount of yarn used by the area.

Imperial: *30 yards ÷ 25 sq. inches = 1.2 yards per sq. inch*

Metric: *27.4 m ÷ 161 sq. cm = 0.17 m per sq. cm)*

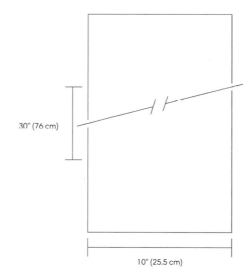

30" (76 cm)

10" (25.5 cm)

Figure 11: *The area of a scarf that measures 10 × 30" (25.5 × 76 cm) is 300 sq. inches (1,938 sq. cm).*

Oval and Out Scarf

DESIGN STRATEGIES

All of the strategies in this section are about yarn management. You have only one ball, with limited yardage, so you'll need to make some decisions to help you use the yardage to its greatest potential.

The Motif Strategy

Projects that Use the Motif Strategy

There are two main methods for one-skein motif projects: Work one large motif or work tons of tiny motifs that you join as you work them.

Think of little motifs as building blocks. You can join the motifs to one another in random order, like patting sand onto a sandcastle. By adding small blocks here and there or adding them in a systematic way, like making a tower, you control the final length and width of the project.

Keep in mind that the building blocks don't have to be square. Hexagons, triangles, and octagons all make great building blocks. Granny squares are the quintessential motif. You can put a bunch of those together to create any shape—blankets, ponchos, tote bags, scarves, cowls. The possibilities are endless when you have versatile building blocks to work with.

Let's see how I applied this strategy to specific projects in this book. Take a look at the Oval and Out Scarf. It may not look like a motif at first, but in fact it is. It's a crocheted piece worked from the inside outward and it can be repeated, although in this project it's just one long, thin motif. Because it's worked in rounds, every round will look great even if

Pentagon Mitts

it becomes the final round. Even if you unexpectedly run out of yarn and have to fasten off, each round is presentable enough to be the final outer border.

The Tumbling Motifs Scarf has motifs connected to one another, but you can't stick them on just any place you like. Each motif progresses off the previous one without cutting. For this reason, it's not a true "join as you go" pattern. It's more like a "progressive motif" pattern. (I'm coining a new term here!) The Tumbling Motifs Scarf uses the motif strategy because it's a unit—a semicircle in this case—and is a repeated shape. You can repeat the semicircle as many times as needed, building onto the previous one, until the yarn is all used up. The idea behind my design was that if your chosen yarn has more yardage than the pattern yarn specifies, you can end according to the pattern or you can keep going until the yarn runs out and a semicircle motif is complete. You can apply the same strategy to your own designs.

The Pentagon Mitts use motifs as the foundation for this pattern. Four identical motifs are repeated for the palms and backs of each hand. Additional stitching is added to turn them into mitts. Each motif uses the same amount of yarn. The project can vary by adding more or less length onto the wrist portion.

Finally, the One Motif Baby Blanket is just one large square motif. It begins like any other motif and only keeps going with more rounds until the yarn runs out.

The joy of the one-motif strategy is that there's no joining and no sewing. The only downside is that subsequent rounds use more and more yarn, making it hard to predict if you'll have enough yarn to complete just one more round!

Narrow as Necessary Scarf

The Narrow-as-Necessary Strategy

Projects that Use the Narrow-as-Necessary Strategy

Oval and Out Scarf, page 40

Narrow as Necessary Scarf, page 44

When working rectangles, it's often the length measurement that's the most important. This is especially applicable to scarves, stoles, cowls, headbands, and ear warmers. When making a headband or ear warmer, for example, the head circumference is the important measurement. Once you have reached that length, the width can be as tall as it needs to be to use up the yarn or complete your vision.

With just one skein that has a small amount of yardage, you might have to compromise on width. The point of this strategy is to make the project as narrow as necessary to get the functionality you need for a successful outcome! You start by achieving the desired length in the first row, then crochet as many rows of width as your yardage allows.

Handled Purse

The No-Sew Strategy

Projects that Use the No-Sew Strategy

When working with only one skein of yarn, the last thing you want is to run out of yarn before assembling the piece together! This would force you to start by holding back some yardage in reserve for sewing a project when the skein has limited yardage, and you don't want to do that. The No-Sew strategy eliminates the need for sewing completely and focuses on designing a project that requires no sewing. Projects that are worked in just one piece without cutting are the best example of no-sew projects. Projects where components are added on as they're worked are also a great example of a no-sew project. No-sew is the way to go!

The Tumbling Motifs Scarf, for example, doesn't require any sewing. The motifs are made progressively without cutting. Because of this, no additional yarn is needed to assemble them together at the end.

If you absolutely can't avoid seaming, you have a choice of two different stitches to connect pieces together. When you're trying to economize on yarn, the seaming method can make a difference. Whipstitch uses less yarn than crocheting pieces together, so use whipstitch instead of crocheting or mattress stitching pieces.

Solomon's Wrap

The Dynamic-Duo Strategy

Projects that Use the Dynamic-Duo Strategy

Locking stitch markers. Placing a locking stitch marker in the working loop will prevent your work from unraveling.

With this strategy, you crochet two of the same items in tandem. Use the Dynamic Duo strategy when you want to make two identical pieces without knowing from the start how big they'll end up being, or you want to make sure they're absolutely the same size. This is the strategy to use for mitts, socks, etc.

To apply this strategy using just one skein or ball of yarn, remove the label and begin one half of the project with the yarn tail that pulls from the center of the skein or ball. At the same time, begin the other half of the project with the yarn tail that unwinds from the outside of the skein or ball. For yarn in a hank, unwind the hank and wind the yarn into a usable center-pull ball (the next page explains how to do that), then work from both the inside of the ball and the outside at the same time.

You should work both pieces at the same time and at the same rate, as follows. You'll need a locking stitch marker.

1. Work about 2 inches (5 cm) on one piece, then put it down, placing a locking stitch marker in the working loop.

2. Then pick up the second half and work the identical amount.

3. Alternate between the two pieces, keeping them even in size and method.

There are exceptions to every rule. The Solomon's Wrap project uses this technique, but in a different way. Instead, the body of this project is worked in one piece from the center of the ball while the outside of the ball is used to work the edging while the wrap is still being stitched.

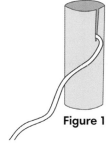

Figure 1

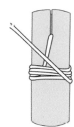

Figure 2

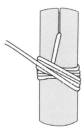

Figure 3

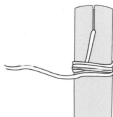

Figure 4

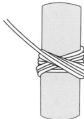

Figure 5

Making a Center-Pull Ball without a Yarn Swift and Ball Winder

You'll need an empty cardboard paper towel tube and scissors.

1. Cut a ¼" (6 mm) slit in the top of the tube. Insert the cut end of the yarn into the slit and keep it there. (That end will be the yarn that feeds from the center of the pull ball.) Flatten the tube in half length-wise (**figure 1**).

2. Wrap the yarn three or four times around the middle of the tube, perpendicular to the tube's axis (**figure 2**).

3. Draw the yarn from the bottom right up to the top left (**figure 3**) then back around the other side to the starting point. You're pulling the yarn up from 5:00 on a clock face up toward 11:00, then back down to 5:00 on the other side; at first, you may have to use your finger to hold the yarn at 11:00. Do this a number of times, making sure that with each turn, the yarn lies beside the previous wrap rather than on top of it (**figure 4**).

4. Next, flip the tube over, and again draw the yarn from 5:00 on a clock face up toward 11:00, then back down to 5:00 on the other side. This will cause these wraps of yarn to crisscross the previous ones. Do this a number of times (**figure 5**), then flip the tube over again.

5. Repeat steps 3 and 4 until you've wound all the yarn around the tube. Then unhook the yarn from the top slit and make sure it stays poking out of the top of the ball. Hold on to the entire ball with your left hand, and use your right one to pull the paper towel tube out from the bottom of the ball.

Coral Reef Scarf

The Divide-and-Conquer Strategy

Projects that Use the Divide-and-Conquer Strategy

Pentagon Mitts, page 52

Coral Reef Scarf, page 74

Like the Dynamic Duo strategy, the Divide and Conquer strategy is also based on the yarn being used in two parts. Whereas the Dynamic Duo strategy uses the yarn from both the inside of the ball and the outside at the same time, the Divide and Conquer strategy separates the yarn into two equal balls before beginning. This saves on any potential tangling and assumes you're working two identical pieces.

When working a yarn ball from both the outside and the center at the same time, the advantage is that you don't have to cut the yarn before you're ready, but it's possible that the yarn can tangle. With the Divide and Conquer strategy, you're forced to cut the yarn in the middle when you separate it into two balls. This is convenient to prevent tangling but then you run the risk of cutting the two balls unevenly and one being smaller than the other.

Here are some methods for splitting yarn into two equal portions.

To divide the yarn on a hank: You'll need a yarn swift and a ball winder. Untwist the hank but leave it tied. Place it on the swift. Count the number of strands. Divide that number by two. Untie the yarn, then wind it while counting until only half the strands are still left on the swift. Cut the yarn, then wind the remainder.

A different approach is to untwist the hank and count the strands. Divide by two. Tie a marker on one spot on the swift itself. Place the hank on the yarn swift. Slowly wind; as you do, count how many times the marker goes around. When it has rotated as many times as the halved number, cut the yarn, then wind the remainder. For example, the yarn for the Coral Reef Scarf started out as 123 strands, and I divided that number by 2 to get 61. I wound until the mark on the swift went around 61 times, then cut the yarn and wound the remainder of the yarn into a second ball.

To divide a ball of yarn: Find the yardage given on the label and divide that number by two. Using any of the methods previously described for measuring yarn (page 10), measure out half of the yardage, and cut the yarn. Re-ball both portions, either with a ball winder or by making a center-pull ball without a yarn swift and ball winder (page 27).

Horizontal Slouch Hat

The Top-Down Strategy

Projects that Use the Top-Down Strategy

The beauty of using the Top-Down strategy when creating a one-skein project is that the length will be determined by the amount of yarn that's available. Hats, ponchos, and sweaters can all be constructed in a top-down manner. It really is possible to make larger projects such as sweaters and ponchos from one skein, but it takes a special touch to get a project like that done with just one ball. It requires employing all the methods of making it lacy, steering clear of sewing, avoiding 3-D texture, and of course starting with a very generous ball of yarn!

Top-down projects are perfect for when extra rows or rounds of stitching could be added at the bottom and still look great or where a shorter length would also work well. For example, the Greenery Hat and the Horizontal Slouch Hat can be made shorter if desired, but if you want to use up the entire skein and have no waste, keep going until the yarn runs out. The hats can then be worn slouchy or you can flip up their brims.

Bruges Wedge Cowl

The Bottoms-Up Strategy

Projects that Use the Bottoms-Up Strategy

Star Stitch Hat, page 66

Bruges Wedge Cowl, page 78

Corner Garden Shawlette, page 88

Market Bag, page 96

The Bottoms-Up strategy is the opposite of the Top-Down strategy and is appropriate for projects on which any excess yarn would look great at the top of the project, either in the form of extra length or as a decorative edge, finish, or flourish. The Star Stitch Hat, for example, starts by making the brim, goes on to stitch up the area that fits around the crown, and finally uses the excess yarn to create a sort of decorative pom-pom flourish at the top. And the Bruges Wedge Cowl is worked in one long piece from the short edge so it can be made longer if you have more yarn yardage.

Because the Corner Garden Shawlette is worked from a beginning point (it's actually shaped kind of like a rhombus), if you chose a different yarn of a longer length, additional rows in the established pattern would make the project both taller and wider.

Corner Garden Shawlette

The Corner-to-Corner Strategy

Projects that Use the Corner-to-Corner Strategy

Coral Reef Scarf, page 74

Corner Garden Shawlette, page 88

Whether you want to make a symmetrical project or prefer the drama of asymmetry, you can make projects that start at one corner and work toward the other. Triangles have half of the area of a rectangular pattern but still span a good usable length to be worn, tied, buttoned, or pinned in place—so in a sense, you can get almost twice the mileage from your skein.

Because the Coral Reef Scarf uses two pieces in the Divide and Conquer method, the results are somewhat predictable. The Corner Garden Shawlette is stitched as one big piece, so it's almost impossible to predict what size the project will turn out if you use a different yarn with a different yardage.

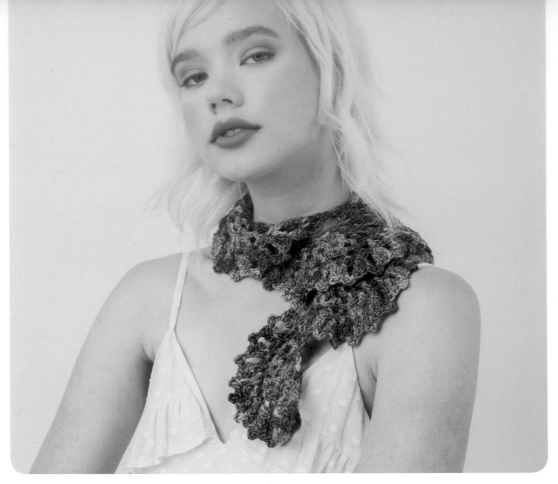

Tumbling Motifs Scarf

The Integrate-the-Edging Strategy

Projects that Use the Integrate-the-Edging Strategy

Making the edging while stitching the body of the project is one of my favorite ways to economize both time and yardage. Most crocheters feel a project is not complete until an edging is in place. By the end of a big project, some stitchers might run out of steam so the edging never gets completed and the project falls into the UFO (UnFinished Objects) bin forever. By crocheting the edging while stitching the body, both pitfalls are avoided. Making the edging as you stitch the main part of the project also maximizes the

yarn because you don't have to overestimate how much yarn to reserve for the edging and possibly cheat yourself of yarn that could have been used for the body of the project. I feel that the edging is the frosting on the cake, but that doesn't mean I have to put it on last. If you work the edging as you stitch and integrate it into the row-by-row or round pattern, when you're finished with the project, the edging is magically complete!

The Oval and Out Scarf, Tumbling Motifs Scarf, and One Motif Baby Blanket feature motifs that have the final round as their edging. In the Coral Reef Scarf, Corner Garden Shawlette, and Narrow as Necessary Scarf, extra stitches added onto the edge of the rows when they're turned function as edging. Whether the edging is fringe-like, as in the Coral Reef Scarf; flower-like, as in the Corner Garden Shawlette; or sweet and tiny, like on the Narrow as Necessary Scarf, you can add these end edge flourishes to any row pattern project you might like to fashion.

Bruges Motif Top

The Lighten-Up Strategy

Projects that Use the Lighten-Up Strategy

Bruges Wedge Cowl, page 78

Bruges Motif Top, page 84

Corner Garden Shawlette, page 88

Market Bag, page 96

Creating a more lacy, open, and airy fabric creates a larger fabric than a solid stitch pattern. For example, in the Coral Reef Scarf, the main body of the scarf is solid stitching. The project could be bigger if chain spaces were introduced to the pattern. Creating effective one-skein projects is all about yarn management and getting the most out of every yard. Chain spaces and lacy stitch patterns make projects look more delicate but mostly they make the overall fabric larger. The Bruges Motif Top is the best example in this book of creating the largest fabric from one skein of yarn.

Greenery Hat

Tips for Maximizing Yardage

Stitches, drape or laciness, and texture are all elements that create a complete project. As you create your unique design, you'll want to consider these concepts. These approaches get the most out of every skein.

Go airy. Solid stitch patterns use up a great deal more yarn than lacy ones, so use lacy stitches as much as possible. If you see that you're using yarn fast and your ball is disappearing at an alarming rate, you might want to make some changes! Changing to a smaller hook size is an option because the stitches will be smaller and use less yarn, but then the overall fabric will be smaller, so it's a trade-off. Another option is to switch mid-project to a more open stitch pattern. Today's trends are all about asymmetry. Changing to a different stitch pattern could add some lovely variety within the project.

Avoid bulky stitches. Stitches like popcorns and dimensional stitches use up more yarn.

Avoid 3-D layering. Don't include things such as post stitches, surface slip stitching, ruffles, and mosaic crochet in your design.

Target the most crucial measurement first. Choose the measurement that's most important and make sure to achieve that first. For example, if you only like scarves that are at least 50" (127 cm) long, work lengthwise to reach the 50" (127 cm) target. You can then work the width row after row until you run out of yarn.

Skip the edging. Keep your work tidy to avoid having to crochet an edging, and save on yarn.

Integrate the edging. Work it as you go so that when you run out of yarn, the edging is already complete and the project is done. The best way to integrate an edging is to do decorative stitches like picots, shells, or fringe on the edge of rows after the row pattern is worked and before the row is turned. Another option is to spread out the edging so that there are stitches that use up more yarn (like picots or clusters) at regular, evenly spaced intervals rather than worked on every stitch or row.

Change the gauge. Simply crocheting a little more tightly will help you eke out a few more stitches when you're playing yarn chicken and may be on the verge of losing. (Yarn chicken is when you try to finish the project before running out of yarn, knowing yarn is running out and it's going to be a close call!) Dropping down a hook size or two might be a solution as well, as long as there isn't a marked difference in appearance of the stitches and you aren't creating puckering with the change in tension.

Build with small join-as-you-go motifs. The Handled Purse uses this strategy. The smaller the motif, the less yardage needed to make each one. Continually add more motifs in any configuration desired to make the project the biggest and best it can be.

Consider the last round of motifs an edging. If you work in motifs, think of every round as potentially an edging. Every round may be your last, because you can only guess when you're going to run out of yarn. Every round uses more yarn than the previous one, making it difficult to predict how much yarn will be used. You can be happy with the finished project if you love every round you make.

Employ asymmetry. Triangles are awesome for scarves and wraps and use up half the yarn of a symmetrical rectangle or square. You can make an asymmetrical scarf by beginning at one point and increasing either on one edge or both edges until the triangle is the desired width. There's no need to decrease back down to a point; allow the asymmetry to be a design feature of the project. Or, when making something like the One Motif Baby Blanket, it's not critical if you can't make it all the way around the final round. Just stop when you run out. It's unlikely anyone will notice it's slightly off balance, and you won't have any leftover yarn.

Additional Considerations for Specific Items

In addition to all the broad choices and assorted strategies you can apply to designing different articles to crochet, there are other things to consider or keep in mind as you're in the beginning stages of the design process.

Scarves. Rectangles are more usable as scarves, cowls, and stoles than squares. The most versatile wrap, scarf, shawl, or cowl begins with a rectangle.

With a scarf, getting the right length is often more important than the width. And when you're limited to just one ball of yarn, creating a scarf that's the right length means you may have to compromise on width.

The Narrow as Necessary Scarf is an example of balancing the length and width of a project. The project uses a very beautiful single hank of yarn that happens to be really short on yardage. Still, we want to not only use the yarn, but use it to its maximum potential. First, I determined the absolute minimum length I was willing to consider for an ascot-type scarf, then worked with the width as a secondary consideration.

The Oval and Out Scarf also used the Narrow as Necessary strategy. I chose a minimum length based on my desire to wrap it around the neck at least once and be able to wear it to fill up the neck opening when wearing a coat. After the length was chosen, then the scarf could be as narrow as needed to make the project a success.

The same concepts apply to a stole or wrap. First determine the length needed to fit and then allow the width to be secondary. A stole can range in length from a shorter stole that you'll wear pinned or buttoned to a longer one that can be tied. When designing your own projects, you get to decide—but at the same time, keep in mind that the bigger the project, the larger that lone skein you're going to crochet it with needs to be to make it happen.

A table runner is shaped much like a scarf. Let's say you want to design one of those. For this type of item, you must consider the length of the table or mantle. Do you want extra length to hang over the edge? Do you want the piece to stop short of the edge? These length considerations will be the first and most important factor.

Back of One Motif Baby Blanket

Cowls. To twist or not to twist? That's the main question when designing a cowl. Should it be long enough to twist and wear two thicknesses around the neck? Should it be smaller and have a twist to add volume? At minimum, a cowl needs to be 21–22" (53.5–56 cm) in diameter or be able to stretch to that size to fit over the head. The maximum length of a cowl is up to you. It can be looped once or twice. More than two loops might be uncomfortable or too crowded to wear.

The ideal height of a cowl is around 8–15" (20.5–38 cm)—that's enough to fill the space between the chin and the opening of a coat. If the stitch pattern is very lacy and open, the cowl will squish more, so you can make the cowl bigger because it will condense down.

Shawls. Shawls come in all shapes and sizes. The possibilities are endless. Rectangles, triangles, semicircles, asymmetrical trapezoids—there are no rules when it comes to shoulder wraps or shawls!

The biggest decision is about width. How wide across the shoulders and wrapping to the front does it need to be? Does it need to tie in front? Will it instead be held with a clasp? The depth of the shawl generally needs to be 15" (38 cm) minimum to cover the back.

Lacy patterns tend to look more formal and dressier. More solid stitch patterns are warmer and thicker. What will you choose?

Blankets. Blankets are a great blank canvas for playing with stitch patterns, color, and texture. There are infinite ways to construct blankets of every size. When designing a blanket, size and expense are two of the most important factors. Of course, with one skein, cost isn't an issue. Is it a blanket that will be throw size for a lap on the couch? Or a cuddle blankie for a toddler?

When it comes to blankets, the yarn must be machine washable. Some designers also take into consideration how "holey" or lacy is the blanket stitch versus how dense and heavy it will be.

Hats. A hat is perhaps one of the more personal gifts that can be crocheted. When I design a hat, I generally start with color. What color are the recipient's eyes? What's his or her favorite color? What color coat would he/she wear it with? What are his/her team or school colors? What style would the recipient like? Beanie? Slouchy? Pom-pom?

Other considerations are the season in which it will be worn. Will it be a sunhat or a winter hat? One with a brim or without? Making hats is fun because it's a low-commitment way to make a fashionable gift and you can make a new one every year! Hats are a great present that can be either trendy and dramatic or functional.

Bags. When designing a bag, it's about function and style combined! Market bags are fantastic for showcasing airy, open stitch patterns that allow for a bit of stretch as the bag is filled with purchases and goodies! Every bag design needs to consider the question of a strap/handle and whether

or not it needs a closure. Other considerations include what type of base or bottom it will have. The base can be a flat piece like a round or oval or rectangular bottom, or the bag can have no real bottom and just be an allover stitch pattern. Depending on the use of the bag, it may need to be lined or not. Instructions for lining a bag with fabric could fill a complete book!

In Summary

In life you sometimes have to throw every possible solution at a tough problem, attacking it on multiple levels. The same is true for fun and hobbies. Having just one skein of yarn in your stash is a problem. (Though not a life-threatening one!) But now I've given you a number of solutions, tips, tricks, and strategies to solve your lonely-skein dilemma. Have fun employing these strategies as you problem-solve a plan for your solo skeins. Just keep in mind: *You* are the master of your stash! *You* determine the destiny of every skein of yarn you buy.

chapter 2
the projects

oval and out
scarf

Super quick to stitch and luxurious in feel, the Oval and Out Scarf solves the question of what to do with a single bulky skein. Interesting, undulating texture will have you inspired to keep stitching!

finished size

3¾ × 51½" (9.5 × 131 cm), blocked.

yarn

112 yards (102 m), bulky weight (#6 Super Bulky).

Shown here: Quince & Co. Puffin (100% American wool; 112 yd [102m]/3.5 oz [100 g]): 142 Sedum, 1 skein.

hook

Size G/6 (4 mm).

Adjust hook size if necessary to obtain correct gauge.

notions

Yarn needle.

gauge

9 sts = 4" (10 cm); 6 rows = 3¾" (9.5 cm).

notes

If you want to change the length, do so in multiples of 6 sts.

Written instructions and stitch diagrams are provided. Use either type alone, or both together as needed.

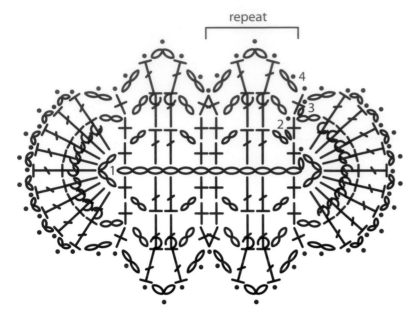

repeat

Key

○	ch
•	sl st
+	sc
†	dc
‡	BPdc

The General Plan

The scarf is made up of a long oval motif worked in turned rounds. Like working an edging, assume every round is your last (because it might be), so make sure you like and work every round as a final round.

Scarf

Rnd 1: (RS) Ch 121, sk 1 ch, *[sc in next ch, ch 2, sk 1 ch, dc in each of next 2 chs, ch 2, sk 1 ch, sc in next ch]* 20 times, ch 4, rotate work to begin working on the underside of the foundation row while RS still faces; rep from * to * 20 times, ch 4; join with sl st in first sc.

Rnd 2: Ch 1, turn, sc in sc, ch 2, 9 dc in ch-4 sp, ch 2, *sc in next sc, ch 2, dc in each of next 2 dc, ch 2, sc in next sc; rep from * across to end, (ch 2, 9 dc) in ch-4 end space, ch 2, **sc in next sc, ch 2, dc in each of next 2 dc***, ch 2, sc in next sc; rep from ** across, ending last repeat at ***, ch 2; join with sl st in first sc.

Rnd 3: Ch 1, turn, sc in sc, [ch 2, BPdc (see Glossary) around next dc] 2 times, *ch 2, sc2tog in next 2 sc, [ch 2, BPdc around next dc] 2 times; rep from * across to end, ch 2, sc in last sc, ch 2 [BPdc around next dc, ch 2] 9 times**, sc in next sc, [ch 2, BPdc (see Glossary) around next dc] 2 times; rep from * once, ending at **; join with sl st in first sc.

Rnd 4: Don't turn, work sl st in every st and ch-2 sp one time around; join with sl st in first st. Fasten off.

Finishing

Weave in ends.

narrow as necessary
scarf

Two narrow twin scarves are joined at two midpoints to create a unique and versatile shape. Ascot in length, the scarf can be tied in multiple ways to create volume or a sleek appearance.

finished size

4½ × 32" (11.5 × 81.5 cm).

yarn

136.5 yards (125 m), sportweight (#2 Fine).

Shown here: Cascade Yarns 220 Superwash Sport (100% superwash Merino wool; 136.5 yd [125 m]/1.75 oz [50 g]): #859 Lake Chelan Heather, 1 skein.

hook

Size G/6 (4 mm).

Adjust hook size if necessary to obtain correct gauge.

notions

Locking stitch markers (m), yarn needle.

gauge

12 rows = 4" (10 cm); 12 sts = 2" (5 cm).

notes

After working Rows 2 and 3, remove the hook and make a slipknot or mark the spot with a barrette, unravel the rows, and measure how much yarn was needed. Take the total yardage of the skein and divide by the amount. This will give the approximate number of repeated rows the skein will yield. Multiply that amount by the row gauge to get an estimate of the length of the finished scarf.

Written instructions and stitch diagrams are provided. Use either type alone, or both together as needed.

Special Stitches

Picot

Ch 3, hdc in 3rd ch from hook.

The General Plan

Working from inside the ball and the outside at the same time, work the two pieces of the scarf in tandem from the short end until the length is reached or until you run out of yarn. Work a picot edging as you go. Once the two pieces are complete, they will be sewn together at the center.

Right Scarf

Working from the inside of the skein or ball.

Row 1: (RS) Ch 13, dc in 4th ch from hook, [ch 2, sk 1 ch, sc in next ch, ch 2, sk 1 ch, dc in next ch] 2 times, dc in final ch, turn. Pm in a RS stitch to mark RS of right scarf.

Row 2: Picot (see Special Stitches), sc in each of next 2 dc, [ch 3, sk sc, sc in next dc] 2 times, sc in final dc, turn.

Row 3: Picot, dc in each of next 2 sc, [ch 2, sc in ch-3 sp, ch 2, dc in next sc] 2 times, dc in final sc, turn. Do not fasten off. Set aside.

Begin working Left Scarf. If necessary, place a locking stitch marker in the loop of the side that is not being worked.

Left Scarf

Working from the outside of the skein or ball, work Rows 1–3 same as Right Scarf. (Do not place a marker in Row 1.)

Work both scarves at the same time.

Rows 4–91: Rep Rows 2 and 3. Fasten off after Row 91.

Work the same number of rows on the right scarf and left scarf. Keep them even.

One will have the wrong side facing up, the other will have the right side facing up. Place them parallel to each other, like snow skis, lining up the ends. Counting picots along the inside edge, with a yarn needle and 1 yd (91.5 cm) of yarn, sew the 6 center picots together that are the 21–26th picots, leaving 20 picots on either side not joined.

Finishing

Weave in ends.

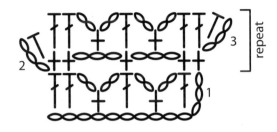
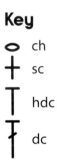

Key

○	ch
†	sc
T	hdc
⊤	dc

tumbling motifs
scarf

Be intrigued by the staggering motifs that seem to defy gravity. These fascinating designs are repeated in a continuous method that becomes addictive! The result is a feminine and floral finish to this ascot-length scarf.

finished size

16 × 25" (40.5 × 63.5 cm).

yarn

150 yards (135 m), DK weight (#3 Light).

Shown here: Manos del Uruguay Silk Blend (70% extrafine Merino wool, 30% silk; 150 yd [137 m]/1.75 oz [50 g]): #3302 Deep Sea, 1 skein.

hook

Size H/8 (5 mm).

Adjust hook size if necessary to obtain correct gauge.

notions

Locking stitch marker, yarn needle.

gauge

Rows 1-6 = 4" (10 cm).

notes

Rows are turned.

You can repeat the motifs as many times as needed, building onto the previous one, until you use up all the yarn. Because of this, if your chosen skein, ball, or hank has more yardage than the yarn specified in the pattern, you can end according to the pattern or you can keep going until the yarn runs out and a motif is complete.

Written instructions and stitch diagrams are provided. Use either type alone, or both together as needed.

Special Stitches

V-stitch (V-st)

(Dc, ch 2, dc) all in st or sp indicated.

Picot

Ch 3, hdc in 3rd ch from hook.

The General Plan

Work stacked and linked motifs until you run out of yarn.

1st Motif

Pm to indicate right side of first motif and leave in place until scarf is complete.

Row 1: (RS) Ch 5; join with sl st in 5th ch from hook to form a ring, ch 4 (counts as first dc plus 1 ch), [dc in ring, ch 1]
6 times, dc in ring, turn—8 dc, 7 ch-1 sps.

Row 2: (WS) Ch 1, sc in first st, [ch 5, sc in next dc] 7 times, turn—8 sc, 7 ch-5 sps.

Row 3: Ch 1 (does not count as a st), V-st (see Special Stitches) in ch-5 sp, [ch 1, V-st in next ch-5 sp] 6 times, turn—7 V-sts, 6 ch-1 sps.

Row 4: Ch 5 (counts as first dc plus 2 chs), [dc in next dc, ch 2] 12 times, dc in last st, turn—14 dc, 13 ch-2 sps.

Row 5: Ch 1, [sc in dc, (sc, ch 3, sc) in ch-2 sp] 13 times, sc in last dc, turn—40 sc, 13 ch-3 sps.

Row 6: Sl st into ch-3 sp, ch 4 (counts as first tr), 2 more tr in same ch-3 sp, [picot (see Special Stitches), 3 tr in next ch-3 sp] 12 times, do not turn—39 tr, 12 picot.

Next Motif

Row 7: Ch 5; join with sl st in 5th ch from hook to form a ring, ch 4 (counts as first dc plus 1 ch), [dc in ring, ch 1] 6 times, dc in ring, sl st in side of previous motif near the base of the last tr set, turn—8 dc, 7 ch-1 sps.

Row 8: Ch 1, sc in first st, [ch 5, sc in next dc] 7 times, turn—8 sc, 7 ch-5 sps.

Row 9: Ch 1 (does not count as a st), V-st in ch-5 sp, [ch 1, V-st in next ch-5 sp] 6 times, sl st in side of previous motif, turn—7 V-sts, 6 ch-1 sps.

Row 10: Ch 5 (counts as first dc plus 2 chs), [dc in next dc, ch 2] 12 times, dc in last st, turn—14 dc, 13 ch-2 sps.

Row 11: Ch 1, [sc in dc, (sc, ch 3, sc) in ch-2 sp] 13 times, sc in last dc, sl st in side of previous motif near the base of Row 2, turn—40 sc, 13 ch-3 sps.

Row 12: Sl st into ch-3 sp, ch 4 (counts as first tr), 2 more tr in same ch-3 sp, [picot, 3 tr in next ch-3 sp] 12 times, do not turn—39 tr, 12 picot.

Repeat next motif to desired length or until you run out of yarn. End at a completed motif (the sample shown on page 48 has eight).

Row 12 (*Optional; this results in a longer scarf and uses more yarn than called for in the materials list, so it's a good choice if you have longer yardage*):
On 3rd through subsequent motifs, on Row 12, sl st into ch-3 sp, ch 4 (counts as first tr), 2 more tr in same ch-3 sp, instead of the first picot, ch 1, sl st in the last picot 2 motifs previous, ch 1, hdc in the ch-1 sp before the sl st (first picot made), 3 tr in next ch-3 sp, [picot, 3 tr in next ch-3 sp] 11 times, turn—39 tr, 12 picot.

Finishing

Weave in ends.

Schematic

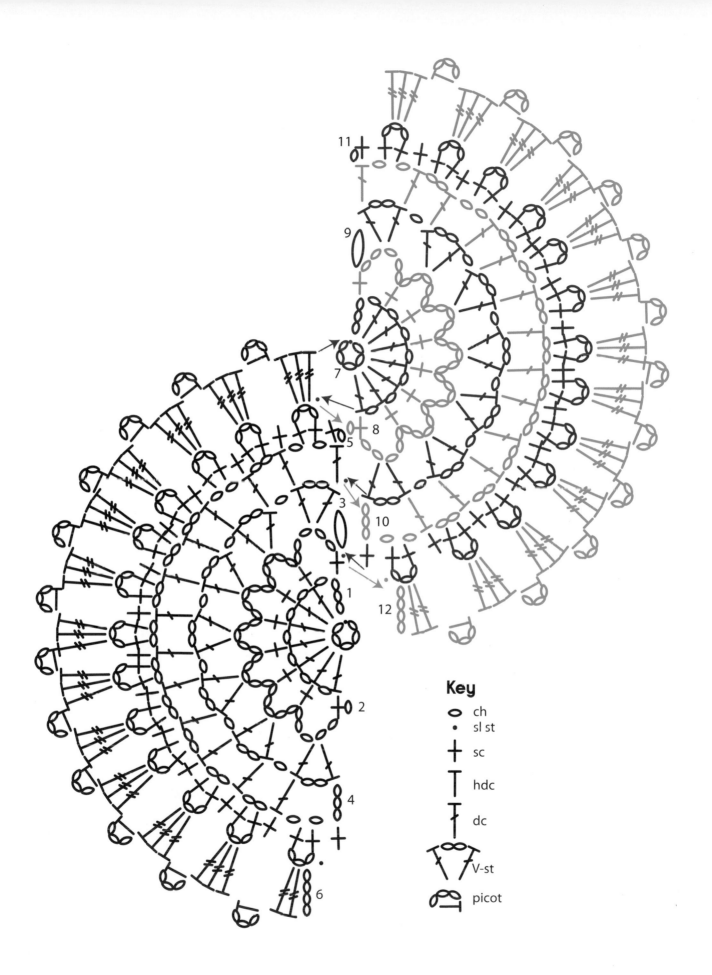

Key

○ ch

• sl st

+ sc

⊤ hdc

⊤ dc

V-st

picot

pentagon
mitts

A five-sided polygon motif is the basis for these clever mitts. Make the motifs that adorn the palm and back of the hand, then add finishing rows. You'll welcome an abundance of warmth and color with this variegated sock yarn.

finished size

Size Small; 3½ × 8½" (9 × 21.5 cm) when flat; 5" (12.5 cm) at widest point.

yarn

166 yards (152 m), sock weight (#1 Super Fine).

Shown here: Patons Kroy Socks FX (75% washable wool, 25% nylon; 166 yd [152 m]/1.75 oz [50 g]): #243457 Celestial Colors, 1 skein.

hook

Size H/8 (5 mm).

Adjust hook size if necessary to obtain correct gauge.

notions

3 locking stitch markers (m), yarn needle.

gauge

Rnds 1–4 = 4" (10 cm), point to point.

notes

Mitts can be made larger as follows: For Size Medium only: Turn and repeat Row 1, one time. For Size Large only: Turn and repeat Row 1, two times.

All rounds are worked on the right side without turning. After the hand sections, the hand sides are seamed and the wrist section is added.

Reserve 3" (7.5 cm) per single crochet (plus slip knot and tail) for seaming. (Mitts in photo are whipstitched.) Whip-stitching takes the least amount of yarn if you're short on fiber.

Written instructions and stitch diagrams are provided. Use either type alone, or both together as needed.

Special Stitches

Beginning 3 Double Crochet Cluster (beg-3-dc-cl)

Ch 3, yo, insert hook in indicated st, yo and pull up lp, yo, draw through 2 lps on hook, yo, insert hook in same st, yo and pull up lp, yo, draw through 2 lps on hook, draw through all 3 lps on hook.

3 Double Crochet Cluster (3-dc-cl)

[Yo, insert hook in indicated st, yo, pull up a lp, yo, pull through 2 lps on hook] 3 times, yo, pull through all 4 lps on hook.

The General Plan

Instead of splitting the ball in two before you begin working, work the two items at the same time. For these mitts, there is a palm side and a back-of-hand side, and then they are seamed. Work the hand portion for each mitt, then you can use up the remaining yarn by adding more rows, alternating working on one mitt then adding rows to the other mitt until the yarn is gone and the mitts are equal.

Hand Section 1 (make 2)

One will be used for the palm of the right hand and the other will be used for the back of the left hand.

Make an adjustable ring (see Glossary).

Rnd 1: (RS) Beg-3-dc-cl (see Special Stitches) in ring, (ch 3, 3-dc-cl [see Special Stitches] in ring) 4 times, ch 1; join with hdc in first cl, do not turn—5 3-dc-cl.

Rnd 2: (RS) Ch 1, sc in same sp as join, [(sc, ch 3, sc) in next 3-dc-cl, (sc, ch 5, sc) in ch-3 sp] 4 times, (sc, ch 3, sc) in next 3-dc-cl, (sc, ch 2) in first ch-3 sp; join with dc in first sc, do not turn—5 ch-5 corner sps, 5 ch-3 sps.

Rnd 3: (RS) Beg-3-dc-cl in sp created by dc join, [ch 1, 3 hdc in ch-3 sp, ch 1, (3-dc-cl, ch 3, 3-dc-cl) in next ch-5 sp] 4 times, ch 1, 3 hdc in ch-3 sp, ch 1, 3-dc-cl in joining dc, ch 1; join with hdc in first 3-dc-cl, do not turn—10 3-dc-cl, 15 hdc.

Rnd 4: (RS) Ch 1, 2 sc in same sp as join, sc in next 3-dc-cl, sc in ch-1 sp, sc in each of next 3 hdc, sc in next ch-1 sp, sc in 3-dc-cl, [5 sc in next ch-3 corner sp, sc in next 3-dc-cl, sc in next ch-1 sp, sc in each of next 3 hdc, sc in next ch-1 sp, sc in next 3-dc-cl] 4 times, 3 sc in last corner sp; join with sl st in first sc, do not turn, do not fasten off—60 sc.

Switch to working in turned rows. Rows do not go all the way around the perimeter.

Note: Row 1 works 3 sides only.

Row 1: (RS) Ch 1 (does not count as a st), dc in same st as join, dc in each of next 10 sc, 3 dc in middle sc of 5-sc corner group, dc in each of next 11 sc, 3 dc in next sc in middle sc of 5-sc corner group, dc in next 12 sc, TURN, leaving remaining stitches unworked—40 dc.

Note: For smaller hands, you can change all the double crochets to single crochets. For larger hands, you can change all the double crochets to treble crochets, but it will use more yarn, so your wrist portion may have to be shorter to compensate.

Row 2: (WS) Ch 1, sc in each of next 13 sts, 3 sc in middle dc of 3-dc group, sc in each of next 13 sts, TURN, leaving remaining sides unworked—29 sc.

These two sides that have the extra single crochets make up the thumb edge and the wrist edge. Fasten off.

Hand Section 1

Palm of Right Hand/
Back of Left Hand

Hand Section 2

Palm of Left Hand/
Back of Right Hand

Key

adjustable ring	
ch	
sl st	
sc	
hdc	
dc	
beg 3-dc-cl	
3-dc-cl	

Hand Section 2 (make 2)

These are the same as for the Hand Section 1 above. One will be used for the back of the right hand and the other will be used for the palm of the left hand.

Note: The right sides should always be facing outward and the extra rows of single crochet go along the thumb and wrist.

Work same as Hand Section 1 through Rnd 4.

Note: Row 1 works 3 sides only.

Row 1: (RS) Ch 1 (does not count as a st), dc in same st, pm in the first dc, dc in next 10 sc, 3 dc in middle sc of 5-sc corner group, dc in next 11 sc, 3 dc in middle sc of 5-sc corner group, dc in next 12 sc, leave remaining stitches unworked. Fasten off—40 dc.

Note: For smaller hands, you can change all the double crochets to single crochets. For larger hands, you can change all the double crochets to treble crochets, but doing so uses more yarn, so your wrist portion may have to be shorter to compensate.

Row 2: With RS facing; join new yarn with sc in the marked st of Row 1, remove the marker, sc in the next 11 sts, 3 sc in middle dc of 3-dc group, sc in each of the next 14 sts, TURN, leaving remaining sides unworked—29 sc.

These two sides that have the extra single crochets make up the thumb edge and wrist edge. Fasten off.

Seam the Two Hand Pieces

With right sides facing each other, seam by whipstitching them along thumb edge toward wrist. Cut yarn and seam down small finger side toward wrist.

Seam gap between thumb and index finger for 11 sts. If needed, try them on and pin the seam in place with locking stitch markers before seaming.

Turn right sides out.

Wrist Section

Rnd 1: Join new yarn with RS facing with dc in the side seam under the thumb, dc in each of the next 29 sts; join with sl st in first dc, do not turn—30 dc.

Note: Try on the mitts. You can increase as needed by placing 2 dc in one stitch. Whatever you do on one mitt, repeat for the other.

To use up the yarn efficiently, work 2 wrist rnds on one mitt then 2 rnds on the other until you run out of yarn and the mitts are even. You can work from both outside and inside the ball at the same time to avoid cutting the yarn and rejoining.

Rnd 2: Ch 1, dc in same st as join and in each st around; join with sl st in first dc, do not turn—30 dc.

Rnds 3–desired length (shown mitts have 10 rnds): Ch 1 (does not count as a st), dc in first st, [FPdc in next st, dc in next st] 14 times, FPdc in next st; join with sl st in first dc, do not turn—30 sts.

Final Rnd: Sl st in each st around. Fasten off.

Sl st around finger opening if desired: With RS facing; join new yarn with sl st in any st and sl st in every st around. Fasten off.

Repeat for second mitt.

Finishing

Weave in ends.

handled

purse

Texture bursts from the surface with dimensional popcorn stitches. Easy hexagonal motifs are joined as they are worked for a no-sew bag body! The handles are crocheted on as the edging is worked for a quick and dramatic finish.

finished size

12" (30.5 cm) wide at base (with corners tucked in), 10½" (26.5 cm) wide at top at opening, 7¾" (19.5 cm) tall.

yarn

170 yards (156 m), worsted weight (#4 Medium).

Shown here: Lion Brand Vanna's Choice (100% acrylic; 170 yd [156 m]/3.5 oz [100g]): #105 Silver Blue, 1 skein.

hook

Size J/10 (6 mm).

Adjust hook size if necessary to obtain correct gauge.

notions

1 pair Blumenthal Purse n-alize-it! bead handbag handles measuring 6.125 × 4.75" (15.5 × 12 cm), yarn needle.

gauge

One motif = 4" (10 cm), point to point.

notes

You will first crochet three vertical rows of motifs, then add the sides.

Written instructions and stitch diagrams are provided. Use either type alone, or both together as needed.

Special Stitches

Beginning Popcorn (beg pc)

Ch 3 (counts as first dc), 2 dc in same sp, remove hook from lp, insert empty hook in the top 2 lps of the first dc/ch 3 of the group, insert the hook also in abandoned working lp, pull the working lp through the top of the first st.

Popcorn (pc)

Place 3 dc in indicated st or sp, remove hook from lp, insert empty hook in the top 2 lps of the first dc of the group, insert the hook also in abandoned working lp, pull the working lp through the top of the first st.

1st Motif

Make an adjustable ring (see Glossary).

Rnd 1: Beg pc (see Special Stitches) in ring, [ch 3, pc (see Special Stitches) in ring] 5 times, ch 3; join with sl st in beg pc—6 pc, 6 ch-3 sps.

Rnd 2: Sl st into ch-3 sp, ch 4 (counts as first tr), 4 more tr (see Glossary) in same sp, [ch 3, 5 tr in next ch-3 sp] 5 times, ch 3; join with sl st in top of first tr, fasten off—30 tr, 6 ch-3 sps.

2nd through 17th Motifs

Rnd 1: Rep Rnd 1 as for 1st Motif.

Rnd 2: Using the schematic on page 61 for guidance, sl st into ch-3 sp, ch 4 (counts as first tr), 4 more tr in same sp, [ch 1, sl st in ch-3 sp of previous motif as necessary, ch 1, 5 tr in next ch-3 sp] 5 times, ch 3; join with sl st in top of first tr, fasten off—30 tr, 6 ch-3 sps.

Top Edging and Handles

Join with single crochet through two lps on one thickness only along top edge. (If you're right-handed, join on the right and work with the bag public/right side facing and work toward the left; if you're left-handed, join on the left and work with the bag public/right side facing and work toward the right). Sc in each st, 3 sc in the ch-3 sps, 1 sc

in ch-3 sp at the top edge, sc twice through the handle loops. Fasten off. Turn bag and repeat for second top edge and second handle. Fasten off and weave in ends.

Fold down the middle top motif and whipstitch it down. Repeat for the opposite one on the other side.

Tuck end corners 2" (5 cm) inward. With yarn and yarn needle, tack corners in their tucked position inside the bag.

Finishing

Weave in ends.

Key

○ ch

๑ adjustable ring

• sl st

† tr

beg pc

pc

Fold top motif in half, to inside bag,
and whipstitch highlighted sides together.

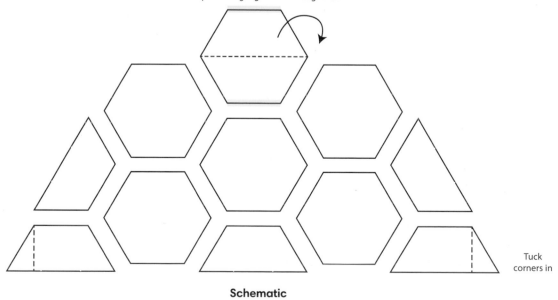

Schematic

Tuck
corners in

greenery
hat

Texture is the crowning feature of this top-down hat. This design was inspired by the generous yardage of the yarn. Adding layering with the pattern maximizes the yarn and creates a thick but flexible finish. Made in superwash Merino wool, this hat will be warm and practical.

finished size

Fits 22" (56 cm) head; crown to brim (measured flat), 8" (20.5 cm).

yarn

186 yards (170 m), worsted weight (#4 Medium).

Shown here: Red Heart Chic Sheep by Marly Bird (100% Merino wool; 186 yd [170 m]/3.5 oz [100g]): #5632 Polo, 1 skein.

hook

Size I/9 (5.5 mm).

Adjust hook size if necessary to obtain correct gauge.

notions

Yarn needle.

gauge

Rnds 1–5 = 4" (10 cm).

notes

Throughout the pattern, the ch 1 at the beginning of a round does not count as a stitch.

Written instructions and stitch diagrams are provided. Use either type alone, or both together as needed.

The General Plan

Work from the crown to the brim until yarn runs out, allowing the hat to be as slouchy as needed to use the yarn completely. When using skeins that have generous yardage, layering stitches, as done in this project, helps use the yarn efficiently without leftovers.

Hat

Make an adjustable ring (see Glossary).

Rnd 1: (RS) h 3 (counts as a dc), 11 dc in ring; join with sl st in first dc—12 dc.

Rnd 2: Ch 1, sc in first st, FPdc (see Glossary) around same st, [sc in next st, FPdc around same st] 11 times; join with sl st in first sc—24 sts.

Rnd 3: Ch 1, sc in first st, *ch 5, sk 1 st, sc in next st; rep from * around, ch 5, sk 1 st; join with sl st in first sc—12 ch-5 lps.

Rnd 4: Working behind the ch-5 sps, ch 1 (does not count as a st), *3 tr (see Glossary) in skipped st 2 rnds previous, ch 1; rep from * around; join with sl st in first tr—36 tr, 12 ch-1 sps.

Rnd 5: Ch 1, sc in same st as join, *pulling up ch-5 lp from 2 rnds previous, sc through it and next tr on working rnd at the same time, sc in next tr, sc in ch-1 sp **; sc in next tr; rep from * around, ending last rep at **; join with sl st in first sc—48 sc.

Rnd 6: Ch 1 (does not count as a st), dc in same st, dc in each st around; join with sl st in first dc.

Rnd 7: Ch 1, sc in same st, *ch 5, sk 1 st, sc in next st; rep from * around, ch 5, sk 1 st; join with sl st in first sc.

Rnd 8: Ch 1 (does not count as a st), working behind the ch-5 sps, [3 tr in each skipped st 2 rnds previous] around; join with sl st in first tr—72 tr.

Rnd 9: Ch 1, sc in same st as join, *pulling up ch-5 lp from 2 rnds previous, sc through it and next tr on working rnd at the same time, sc in next 2 sts; rep from * around, ending last repeat with 1 sc; join with sl st in first sc—72 sc.

Rnds 10 and 11: Rep Rnds 6 and 7.

Rnd 12: Ch 1, [2 tr in each skipped st 2 rnds previous] around; join with sl st in first tr.

Rnd 13: Ch 1, sc in same st, *pulling up ch-5 lp from 2 rnds previous, sc through it and next tr on working rnd at the same time**, sc in next st; rep from * around , ending last rep at **; join with sl st in first sc—72 sc.

Rnds 14-25: [Rep Rnds 10-13] 3 times.

Rnd 26: Ch 1, *sc in each of the next 7 sts, sc2tog; rep from * around; join with sl st in first sc. Fasten off.

Finishing

Weave in ends.

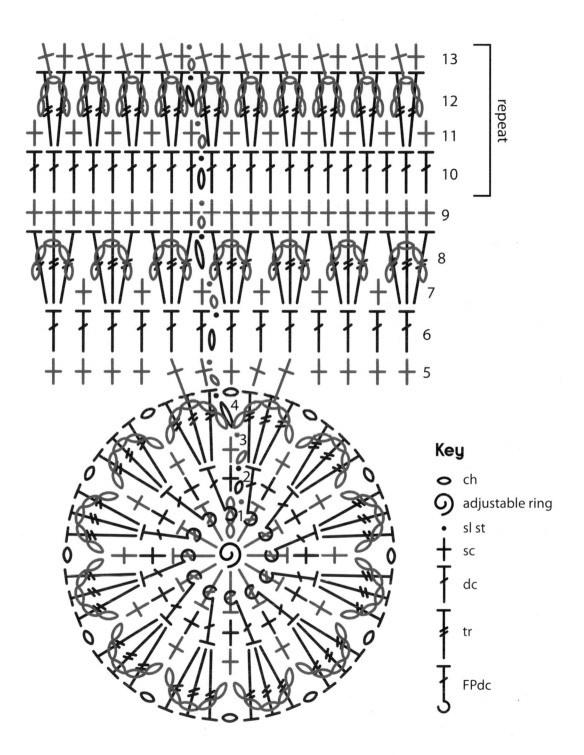

Key

⟨ ⟩ ch	ch
⟨ ⟩ adjustable ring	adjustable ring
• sl st	sl st
+ sc	sc
┼ dc	dc
‡ tr	tr
FPdc	FPdc

star stitch
hat

Variegated yarns shine with the star stitch in this funky brim-up hat. Take the star stitch further with decreasing to create the perfect colorful beanie with amazing thickness and warmth. Eliminate the top few rounds to leave it open for a ponytail!

finished size

Fits 21½" (54.5 cm) head circumference; total height 9½" (24 cm).

yarn

197 yards (180 m), worsted weight (#4 Medium).

Shown here: Universal Yarn Classic Shades (70% acrylic, 30% wool; 197 yd [180 m]/3.5 oz [100g]): #711 Grapevine, 1 skein.

hook

Size I/9 (5.5 mm).

Adjust hook size if necessary to obtain correct gauge.

notions

Locking stitch marker (m), yarn needle.

gauge

8 stars and 10 rows = 4" (10 cm).

notes

Hat is worked from brim up toward crown.

Written instructions and stitch diagrams are provided. Use either type alone, or both together as needed.

Special Stitches

Foundation Single Crochet (fsc)

First foundation single crochet: Ch 2, insert hook into 2nd ch from hook, yo, pull up a lp, yo, pull through 1 lp on hook (ch made), yo, pull through both lps on hook.

Next foundation single crochet: [Insert hook in last ch made, yo, pull up a lp, yo, pull through 1 lp on hook, yo, pull through both lps on hook] repeat as many times as indicated in instructions.

Star Stitch (star)

Insert hook into eyelet just formed, yo and draw up a lp, insert hook into final post st of last star made, yo and draw up a lp, insert hook into each of next 2 sts on row and draw up a lp (5 lps on hook), yo and pull through all lps on hook, ch 1 (eyelet made).

Star decrease (star dec)

Insert hook into eyelet just formed and draw up a lp, insert hook into final post st of last star made and draw up lp, insert hook into next st, sk 1 st, insert hook into next st on row and draw up a lp (5 lps on hook), yo and pull through all lps on hook, ch 1 (eyelet made).

The General Plan

Starting at the brim, decrease until the desired slouchiness is reached. Add a fluffy few rows and tie for decoration. To use up more yarn, add more rounds by repeating Rnd 13.

Hat

Fsc (see Special Stitches) 83, taking care not to twist; join with sl st in first st to form a circle.

Rnd 1: (RS) Ch 2, work stars (see Special Stitches) all the way around, do not join at the end of Rnd 1. Mark first star with locking stitch marker and move up as work progresses—41 stars.

Rnds 2-7: Continue working in a spiral, make star using eyelets, top of beg ch-2, then next 2 sts.

Note: On Rnds 2-7, when working even, the last pull up of every star pulls up in an eyelet.

Rnd 8: *Work 3 stars, star dec (see Special Stitches) once; rep from * around, finish with 1 extra star—37 stars.

Rnd 9: Work even.

Rnd 10: Rep Rnd 8—33 stars.

Rnd 11: Work even.

Rnd 12: Rep Rnd 8—30 stars.

Rnd 13: Work even.

Rnd 14: Rep Rnd 8, finish with 3 extra stars—27 stars.

Rnd 15: Rep Rnd 8—24 stars.

Rnd 16: Rep Rnd 8, finish with 1 extra star—21 stars.

Rnd 17: *Work 2 stars, star dec once; rep around—18 stars.

Rnd 18: Rep Rnd 17, finish with 1 extra star—16 stars.

Rnd 19: Rep Rnd 17—11 stars.

Rnd 20: (Tie rnd) Ch 4 (counts as first dc plus ch-1 sp), *sk 1 st, dc in next st, ch 1; rep from * around; join with sl st in 3rd ch of beg ch-4—11 dc, 11 ch-1 sps.

Rnd 21: Ch 1 (does not count as a st), working in front lp only, 3 dc in each ch and st around; join with sl st in first dc—66 dc.

Rnd 22: Ch 4 (counts as first tr), working in unused back lp only of Rnd 20, 2 tr in first st, 3 tr in each ch around; join with sl st in first tr—66 tr.

Fasten off.

Weave in ends.

Tie

Ch 101, sl st in 2nd ch from hook and in each ch across—100 sl st.

Fasten off. Weave through ch-1 sps of Rnd 20. Tie in a bow.

Finishing

Edging: Join new yarn with sc in any stitch on brim under the foundation chain, *ch 1, sc in next st; rep from * around; join with sl st in first st. Fasten off.

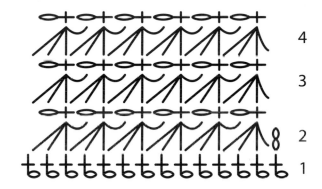

Key

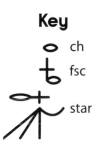

○ ch

ᵗ fsc

⋆ star

horizontal slouch
hat

Eye-catching horizontal banding is created with a fun and easy slip stitch method and turned rows. The textural stripes add dimension in this rich solid yarn. This hat can be worn slouchy or has more of a beanie shape if the brim is turned up.

finished size

Fits 21" (53.5 cm) head circumference; crown to brim (measured flat), 9" (23 cm).

yarn

218 yards (199 m), worsted weight (#4 Medium).

Shown here: Berroco Vintage (52% acrylic, 40% wool, 8% nylon; 218 yd [199 m]/3.5 oz [100g]): #5173 Red Pepper, 1 skein.

hook

Size I/9 (5.5 mm).

Adjust hook size if necessary to obtain correct gauge.

notions

Locking stitch marker (m), yarn needle.

gauge

33 sts and 14 rows = 4" (10 cm) in pattern.

notes

Half the rounds are worked on the right side without turning. Some rows are turned and worked on the wrong side.

If you use the yarn listed in these instructions and achieve gauge, you'll only have 1 yard (91 cm) left over once finished, so don't feel nervous as you near the end of the pattern.

Written instructions and stitch diagrams are provided. Use either type alone, or both together as needed.

Special Stitches

Double Slip Stitch (dsst)

Double slip stitch is worked on the wrong side.

First st: Insert the hook in the first st, pull up a lp and leave it there, pull up a lp in the next st and pull it through the fabric and through all lps on the hook.

2nd and subsequent sts: Insert the hook in the last st that was just used, yo and pull up a lp through the fabric, insert the hook in the next unused st, yo and pull through the fabric and through all lps on the hook.

The General Plan

Work from the crown to the brim until yarn runs out, allowing the hat to be as slouchy as needed to use the yarn completely. You can fold up the brim for comfort.

Hat

Rnd 1: (RS) Ch 3, 15 dc in 3rd ch from hook; join with sl st in top first dc—16 dc.

Rnd 2: (RS) Ch 3 (counts as first dc), dc in same st, 2 dc in each rem st around; join with sl st in first dc—32 dc.

Rnd 3: (RS) Ch 1 (does not count as a st), FPdc (see Glossary) around each st around; join with sl st in first FPdc—32 FPdc.

Rnd 4: (RS) Ch 1 (does not count as a st), working in back lps only, 2 dc in each st around; join with sl st in first st—64 dc.

Rnds 5 and 6: (RS) Rep Rnd 3.

Rnd 7: (WS) Turn, work the opposite direction with the WS facing, working in front lp only, dsst (see Special Stitches) around, do not join, work in a spiral.

Rnd 8: (WS) Do not turn, continue with the WS facing, pm in first st to mark the beginning of the rnd, continue working in front lp only, dsst in each st around, do not join.

Rnd 9: (RS) Turn, work the opposite direction of the previous rnd. The RS is now facing. Working in the back lp only, ch 1 (does not count as a st), *dc in each of next 7 sts, 2 dc in next; rep from * around; join with sl st in first st—72 dc.

Rnds 10 and 11: (RS) Do not turn, continue with the RS facing, ch 1, FPdc around each st around; join with sl st in first FPdc—72 FPdc.

Rnds 12-31: Rep Rnds 7-11 until you run out of yarn. Fasten off. If recommended yarn was used and given gauge was achieved, 220 yards finished at Rnd 31.

Finishing

Weave in ends.

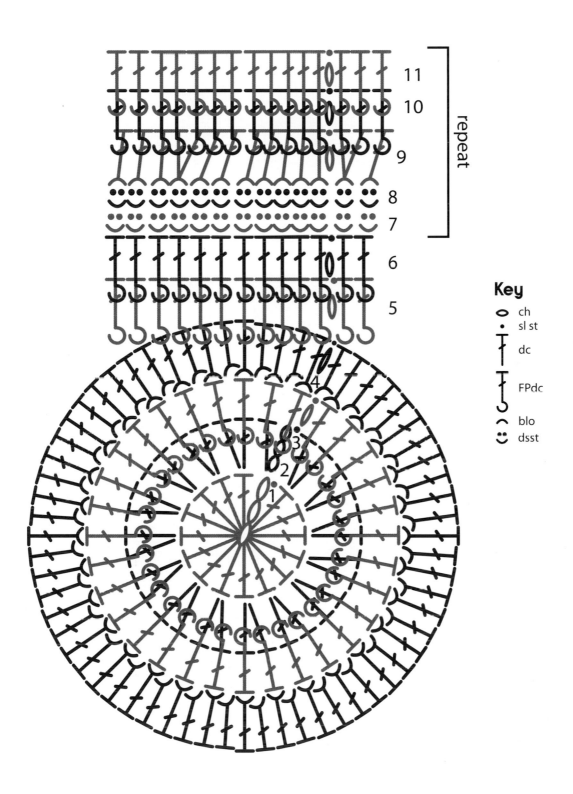

Key

◦	ch
•	sl st
†	dc
┬	FPdc
⌒	blo
☺	dsst

coral reef
scarf

Modern and dynamic, this scarf is just as fun to stitch as to wear! Split the yarn in two and make twin pieces joined with a simple lattice-style join. The yarn does all the color work with beginner stitching for the body and an easy integrated fringe for the edging.

finished size

48 × 7½" (122 × 19 cm), excluding fringe.

yarn

220 yards (200 m), worsted weight (#4 Medium).

Shown here: Cascade Yarns 220 Superwash Wave (100% superwash wool; 220 yd [200 m]/3.5 oz [100g]): #113 Unicorn, 1 skein.

hook

Size I/9 (5.5 mm).

Adjust hook size if necessary to obtain correct gauge.

notions

Locking stitch marker (m), yarn needle.

gauge

15 sts and 8 rows = 4" (10 cm).

notes

Work one half and fasten off. Work the second half identically to the first but join on the final row.

Written instructions and stitch diagrams are provided. Use either type alone, or both together as needed.

The General Plan

You'll increase on every RS row but only along one edge. Work fringe on the edge where the increases are placed. To make fringe, ch 9, sl st in second ch from hook and in remaining 7 chs for a total of 8 sl sts.

This pattern uses the Divide and Conquer technique, so you'll start by dividing the skein into two equal lengths and work from one point until the yarn is used. This edge will become the middle of the scarf once both halves are joined. Pull back on one piece as necessary until the two pieces are equal and have an odd number of stitches. Save enough yarn to make one row of ch-5 lps.

Page 28 describes a variety of methods for dividing yarn.

1st Half

Row 1: (RS) Ch 4, 2 dc in 4th ch from hook (3 skipped chs count as first dc)—3 dc.

Row 2: Ch 9, (place marker in 9th ch and leave it there throughout the whole process to indicate that is the edge where increases will happen), turn, sl st in 2nd ch from hook and in each of next 7 chs across, 2 dc in first dc, dc in each dc across.

Row 3: Ch 3 (does not count as a st), turn, dc in each dc across.

Row 4: Ch 9, turn, sl st in 2nd ch from hook and in each of next 7 chs across, 2 dc in first dc, dc in each dc across.

Rows 5-48: Repeat Rows 3 and 4.

Row 49: Repeat Row 3.

Row 50 (1st Half only): Ch 9, turn, sl st in 2nd ch from hook and in each of next 7 chs, *sc in next dc, ch 5, sk 1 dc; rep from * across, sc in final st. Fasten off.

2nd Half

Repeat Rows 1-49 for the 2nd Half of the scarf using the second portion of yarn.

Row 50 (2nd Half only): Ch 9, turn, sl st in 2nd ch from hook and in next 7 ch, *sc in next dc, ch 2, sl st in corresponding ch-5 sp of 1st Half, ch 2, sk 1 dc; rep from * across, sc in final st. Fasten off.

Finishing

Weave in ends.

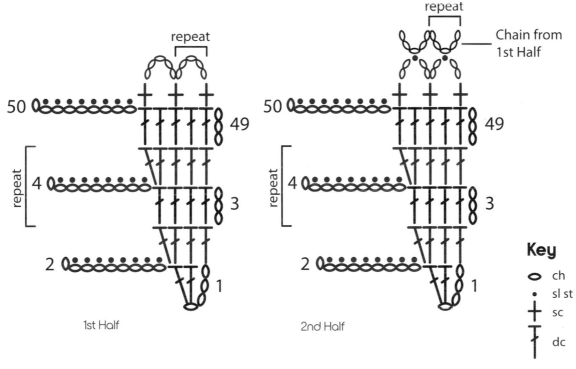

repeat

repeat

Chain from
1st Half

50

49

repeat

4

3

2

1

1st Half

50

49

repeat

4

3

2

1

2nd Half

Key

○ ch

• sl st

┼ sc

┼ dc

bruges wedge
cowl

Simple stitching is so exciting in the Bruges Lace technique! The airy fabric it creates makes the yarn go farther. The chain loops at the end of rows add laciness and interest in between sections of double crochet. The join-as-you-go triangular motifs add dynamic flair to this easy-to-stitch cowl.

finished size

7 × 21" (18 × 53.5 cm) when folded in half as a cowl, 7 × 42" (18 × 106.5 cm) before seaming.

yarn

250 yards (228 m), DK weight (#3 Light).

Shown here: Anzula Cricket (80% superwash Merino wool, 10% Cashmere, 10% nylon; 250 yd [228 m]/4.02 oz [114g]): Mauve, 1 skein.

hook

Size I/9 (5.5 mm).

Adjust hook size if necessary to obtain correct gauge.

notions

Locking stitch marker (m), yarn needle.

gauge

Rows 1–16 = 6½" (16.5 cm); 8 sts = 2" (5 cm).

One wedge: 16 rows = 6½" (16.5 cm).

notes

Rows are turned.

Written instructions and stitch diagrams are provided. Use either type alone, or both together as needed.

Special Stitches

Double Treble Crochet (dtr)

Yo 3 times, insert hook into indicated st or sp, yo and pull up a lp, [yo and pull through 2 lps on hook] 4 times.

The General Plan

Work from the short end until the length is reached or until you have only 8 yards (7.3 m) of yarn left—each side requires 4 yards (3.7 m) for the edging. Or omit the edging altogether.

1st Wedge

Row 1: (RS) Ch 6, 3 dc in 6th ch from hook—3 dc.

Row 2: (WS) Ch 5, turn, dc in each of next 3 dc—3 dc.

Row 3: Ch 5, turn, 2 dc in first dc, dc in each dc across—4 dc.

Row 4: Ch 5, turn, dc in each dc across.

Row 5: Ch 5, turn, 2 dc in first dc, dc in each dc across—5 dc.

Row 6: Ch 5, turn, dc in first dc, *ch 1, sk next st, dc in next dc; rep from * across.

Row 7: Ch 5, turn, 2 dc in first dc, dc in each ch and dc across—6 dc.

Row 8: Ch 5, turn, dc in each dc across.

Row 9: Ch 5, turn, 2 dc in first dc, dc in each dc across—7 dc.

Row 10: Rep Row 6.

Row 11: Rep Row 7—8 dc.

Row 12: Rep Row 8.

Row 13: Rep Row 9—9 dc.

Row 14: Rep Row 6.

Row 15: Rep Row 7—10 dc.

Row 16: Rep Row 8. Turn. Pm in ch-5 loop at beg of row.

2nd Wedge

Row 1: Ch 8, 2 dc in 4th ch from hook (makes the point on the next wedge).

Row 2: Ch 2, sl st in next available ch-5 side lp, ch 2, turn, dc in each dc across.

Row 3: Ch 5, turn, 2 dc in first dc, dc in each dc across—4 dc.

Row 4: Rep 2nd Wedge Row 2.

Row 5: Rep 2nd Wedge Row 3—5 dc.

Row 6: Ch 2, sl st in next available ch-5 side lp, ch 2, turn, dc in first dc, *ch 1, sk 1 st, dc in next dc; rep from * across.

Row 7: Ch 5, turn, 2 dc in first dc, dc in each ch and dc across—6 dc.

Row 8: Rep 2nd Wedge Row 2.

Row 9: Rep 2nd Wedge Row 3—7 dc.

Row 10: Rep 2nd Wedge Row 6.

Row 11: Rep 2nd Wedge Row 7—8 dc.

Row 12: Rep 2nd Wedge Row 2.

Row 13: Rep 2nd Wedge Row 3—9 dc.

Row 14: Rep 2nd Wedge Row 2.

Row 15: Rep 2nd Wedge Row 3—10 dc.

Row 16: Dtr (see Special Stitches) in the ch-5 lp of Row 1 of the 1st Wedge, turn, (do not ch) dc in each dc across.

3rd–19th Wedges

Rep 2nd Wedge 17 times.

20th (Final) Wedge

As this wedge is worked, it is joined to the 1st Wedge to form a tube.

Row 1: Ch 6, sl st in first marked lp from 1st Wedge in Row 16, ch 2, turn, sk ch-2 sp just made, sk next 3 ch, 3 dc in next ch—3 dc.

Row 2: Ch 2, sl st in next available ch-5 lp on 19th Wedge, ch 2, turn, dc in each dc across.

Row 3: Ch 2 (does not count as a st), sl st in ch-5 lp on 1st Wedge, turn, 2 dc in first dc, dc in each dc across—4 dc.

Row 4: Rep 20th Wedge Row 2.

Row 5: Rep 20th Wedge Row 3—5 dc.

Row 6: Ch 2, sl st in next available ch-5 side lp on 19th wedge, ch 2, turn, dc in first dc, *ch 1, sk 1 st, dc in next dc; rep from * across.

Row 7: Ch 2, sl st in next ch-5 lp on 1st Wedge, turn, 2 dc in first dc, dc in each ch and dc across—6 dc.

Row 8: Rep 20th Wedge Row 2.

Row 9: Rep 20th Wedge Row 3—7 dc.

Row 10: Rep 20th Wedge Row 6.

Row 11: Rep 20th Wedge Row 7—8 dc.

Row 12: Rep 20th Wedge Row 2.

Row 13: Rep 20th Wedge Row 3—9 dc.

Row 14: Rep 20th Wedge Row 6.

Row 15: Rep 20th Wedge Row 7—10 dc.

Row 16: Dtr in the base of the first row of the previous wedge (where the first 3 dc of that wedge are worked), turn, (do not ch) dc in each dc across, tr (see Glossary) in base of 3-dc group of first wedge. Fasten off.

Edging

Row 1: (RS) Join with sc in first dc of any 10-dc section along outside edge of cowl, *[ch 3, sk 2 dc, sc in next st] 3 times, ch 3, sk next 2 side sps, sc in ch at base of next wedge, ch 3, sk next ch-sp**, sc in next dc; rep from * around, ending last rep at **; join with sl st in first sc. Fasten off.

Repeat for opposite edge.

Finishing

Weave in ends.

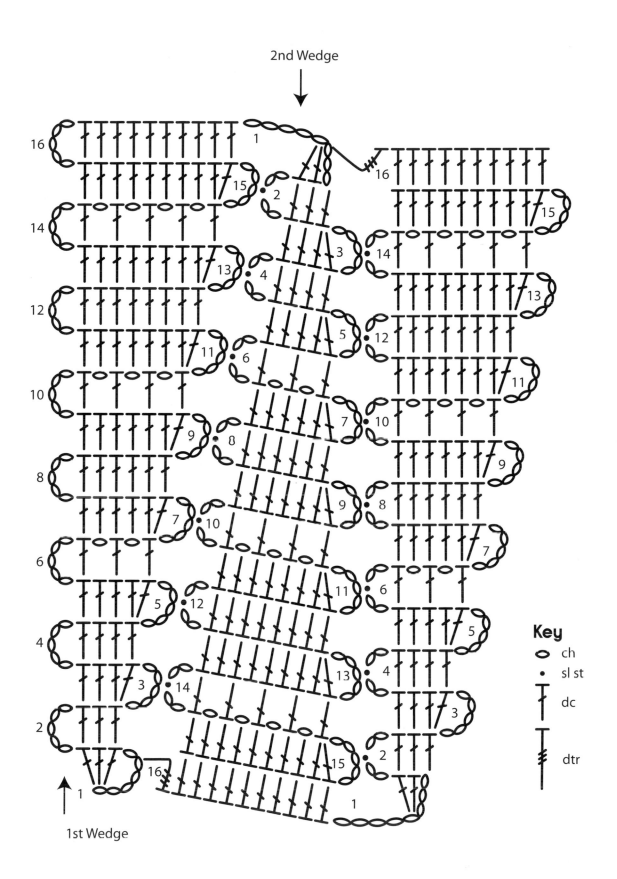

2nd Wedge

1st Wedge

Key

- ◯ ch
- • sl st
- † dc
- ‡ dtr

bruges motif

top

Easy Bruges-style motifs are made with basic crochet stitches in this airy and mesmerizing top! Motifs are joined as they are worked for a no-sew finish.

finished size

12 × 18" (30.5 × 45.5 cm), fits bust circumference up to 36" (91.5 cm).

yarn

255 yards (233 m), DK weight (#3 Light).

Shown here: Skacel HiKoo Sueño (80% superwash Merino wool, 20% viscose from bamboo; 255 yd [233 m]/3.5 oz [100g]): #1164 Slated, 1 skein.

hook

Size G/6 (4 mm).

Adjust hook size if necessary to obtain correct gauge.

notions

Locking stitch marker (m), yarn needle.

gauge

One motif = 4" (10 cm), before blocking.

notes

This yarn grows significantly when wet-blocked. Item is shown after blocking. If a different yarn is used, results will vary substantially.

Join-as-you-go motifs can be placed in any configuration to make endless projects. To maximize a ball of yarn, use smaller motifs and keep adding until the yarn runs out.

Written instructions and stitch diagrams are provided. Use either type alone, or both together as needed.

Motif (32 total)

Row 1: Leaving a 3" (7.5 cm) tail, ch 9, dc in 6th ch from hook, ch 2, sk 2 chs, sc in last ch.

Row 2: Ch 1, turn, sc in first sc, ch 2, sk 2 chs, dc in dc.

Row 3: Ch 5, turn, dc in first dc, ch 2, sk 2 sts, sc in sc.

Rows 4-15: Rep Rows 2 and 3.

Row 16: Rep Row 2.

Do not fasten off. With yarn needle and beginning tail, sew Row 1 to Row 16. Continue to Join Round.

Join Round

1st motif only:

Rnd 1: Sl st into ch-5 sp of Row 1, ch 1, sc in same lp, *ch 7**; sc in next outer ch-5 lp; rep from * around, ending last rep at **; join with sl st in first sc. Fasten off.

1-side-join motif only:

Rnd 1: Sl st into ch-5 sp of Row 1, ch 1, sc in same lp, ch 3, sl st in adjacent ch-5 lp of other motif (refer to schematic for placement), ch 3, sc in next outer lp on current motif, ch 3, sc in adjacent ch-5 lp of same motif, ch 3, sc in next outer lp on current motif, *ch 7**; sc in next outer ch-5 lp; rep from * around, ending last rep at **; join with sl st in first sc. Fasten off.

2-side-join motif only:

Rnd 1: Sl st into ch-5 sp of Row 1, ch 1, sc in same lp, ch 3, sl st in adjacent ch-5 lp of other motif (refer to schematic for placement), ch 3, sc in next outer lp on current motif, ch 3, sc in adjacent ch-5 lp of same motif, ch 3, sc in next outer lp on current motif, *ch 7, in next outer ch-5 lp; rep from * 3 times, ch 3, sl st in adjacent ch-5 lp of other motif (refer to schematic for placement), ch 3, sc in next outer lp on current motif, ch 3, sl st in adjacent ch-5 lp of same motif, ch 3; join with sl st in first sc. Fasten off.

Following instructions for 1-side-join motif or 2-side-join motif, join each motif to subsequent motifs so that a tube made up of 3 rows of 10 motifs each is formed, then attach two motifs to form the shoulder and bring in the neckline. For more details on overall construction, refer to the schematic.

Waist/Hem Edging

Row 1: With new yarn, ch 8, tr in the 6th ch from hook and in next 2 ch, ch 2; join with sl st into an unused ch-7 sp of a motif.

Row 2: Ch 2, turn, tr in first tr, ch 1, sk 1 tr, tr in next tr.

Row 3: Ch 5, turn, tr in first tr, ch 1, sk 1 ch, tr in next tr, ch 2; join with sl st in next unused ch-7 sp of same motif.

Rows 4-79: Rep Rows 2 and 3 all the way around, skipping the spaces where motifs are joined.

Row 80: Rep Row 2. Fasten off, leaving a 4" (10 cm) tail. With yarn needle, sew Row 80 to Row 1.

Neckline Edging

Join new yarn with sc in any ch-sp, *ch 5, sc in next ch-sp; rep from * around; join with sl st in first sc. Fasten off.

Weave in all ends.

Finishing

Wet block gently. Dry flat on towels; hanging to dry will distort the shape.

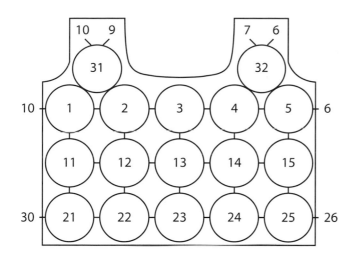

Although the top consists of 32 motifs, this schematic shows only one side of the top, which is why some numbers aren't shown; the motifs on the other side connect in the same way.

Shoulder Motifs (motifs 31 and 32): *One motif crosses each shoulder. The numbers above the circles indicate which motif from Row 1 to join each shoulder motif with.*

Row 1 (motifs 1–10): *The motifs at the ends connect to 5 joined motifs on the other side.*

Row 2 (motifs 11–20): *The 5 motifs on this side connect to the motifs in Rows 1 and 3, but not to the 5 motifs on the other side; this creates an armhole.*

Row 3 (motifs 21–30): *The motifs at the ends connect to 5 joined motifs on the other side.*

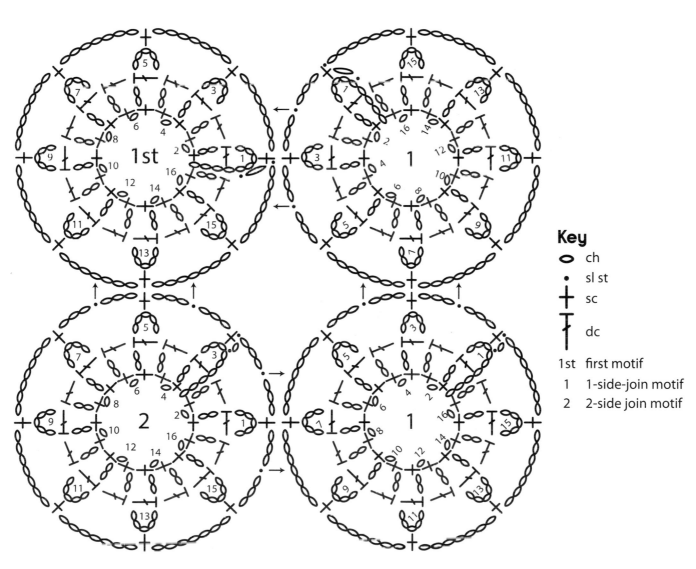

Key

○ ch

• sl st

✝ sc

 dc

1st   first motif

1   1-side-join motif

2   2-side join motif

corner garden
shawlette

The versatile diamond shape of this intermediate mini cowl is fun and interesting to work! Laciness is added to help the yarn stretch farther. Integrating the edging creates a fun flourish on the edges that resembles tiny butterflies.

finished size

16½ × 14½" (42 × 37 cm) deep at center point; when folded in half, 33 × 14½" (84 × 37 cm).

yarn

275 yards (251 m), DK weight (#3 Light).

Shown here: Lorna's Laces Honor (70% baby alpaca, 30% silk; 275 yd [251 m]/ 3.5 oz [100 g]): #117 Atticus, 1 skein.

hook

Size H/8 (5 mm).

Adjust hook size if necessary to obtain correct gauge.

notions

Yarn needle, one ½" (1.3 cm) button (optional).

gauge

18 sts and 11 rows = 4" (10 cm).

notes

Work until you run out of yarn and a row is completed.

In general, the pattern is worked two solid rows, then one mesh row.

Edge leaf is worked at the beginning and end of a mesh row only.

The pattern increases on every edge, then is worked one for one to the point. Half of the stitches to the point will be dc, then the second half of the stitches to the point will be esc, until you reach row 20.

Then all remaining rows will only have 20 dc, and the balance to the point are all esc.

At the point always work (esc, ch 2, esc) in the ch-2 sp.

Written instructions and stitch diagrams are provided. Use either type alone, or both together as needed.

Special Stitches

Extended Single Crochet (esc)

Insert hook in next st, yo and pull up a lp, yo, pull through 1 lp on hook, yo, pull through remaining 2 lps on hook.

Edge Leaf (edge leaf)

Ch 4, turn, 3 dc in 4th ch from hook, ch 3, sk 3 chs, place 3 dc around post of the 3rd dc of the group just made.

The General Plan

Work one large motif in a similar manner as a chevron until you run out of yarn. Work the edging simultaneously.

Shawlette

Row 1: (RS) Ch 4, (dc, ch 2, 2 dc) in 4th ch from hook (2 skipped chs count as first dc), turn.

Row 2: Ch 1 (does not count as a st), 2 dc in first dc, esc (see Special Stitches) in next dc, (esc, ch 2, esc) in ch-2 sp, esc in next st, 2 dc in last st, turn.

Row 3: Work edge leaf (see Special Stitches), 2 dc in first st, ch 1, sk 1 st, dc in next st, ch 1, (esc, ch 2, esc) all in ch-2 sp, ch 1, sk 1 st, dc in next st, ch 1, 2 dc in final stitch, work edge leaf, turn.

Row 4: Ch 1 (does not count as a st), 2 dc in first dc, dc in next st and ch, esc in each st and ch to point, (esc, ch 2, esc) in ch-2 sp, esc in each st to last ch, dc in next ch and next st, 2 dc in final st, turn.

Row 5: Ch 1 (does not count as a st), 2 dc in first dc, dc in each of the next 3 sts, esc in each st to point, (esc, ch 2, esc) in ch-2 sp, esc in each st to the last 4 sts, dc in the next 3 sts, 2 dc in final st, turn.

Row 6: Work edge leaf, 2 dc in first st, *ch 1, sk 1 st, dc in next st*; rep bet * across to ch-2 sp, at ch-2 sp ch 1, (esc, ch 2, esc) all in ch-2 sp, rep bet * across to last st, working 2 dc in final stitch, work edge leaf, turn.

Rows 7-18: [Rep Rows 4–6] 4 times, making sure the number of double crochets on each side of the point match the number of the row.

Rows 19 and 20: Repeat Rows 4 and 5.

Row 21: Rep Row 3.

Rows 22 and 23: Ch 1 (does not count as a st), 2 dc in first dc, dc in each of the next 18 sts, esc in each st to point, (esc, ch 2, esc) in ch-2 sp, esc in each st to the last 19 sts, dc in the next 18 sts, 2 dc in final st, turn.

Note: At this point, there will be 20 dcs on each side of the center ch-2 sp.

Row 24: Rep Row 3.

Rows 25-36: [Rep Rows 22–24] 4 times.

Row 37: Rep Row 22.

Row 38: Sl st in each st and ch across with only 1 sl st in ch-2 point space.

Optional: Tack the points with yarn to be worn as a cowl/tube (shown).

Also optional: If desired, sew a 1/2" (1.3 cm) button between Rows 34 and 35 on RS about 5 stitches in from edge (not shown).

Finishing

Weave in all ends.

Key

- o ch
- + sc
- ⊤ dc
- esc

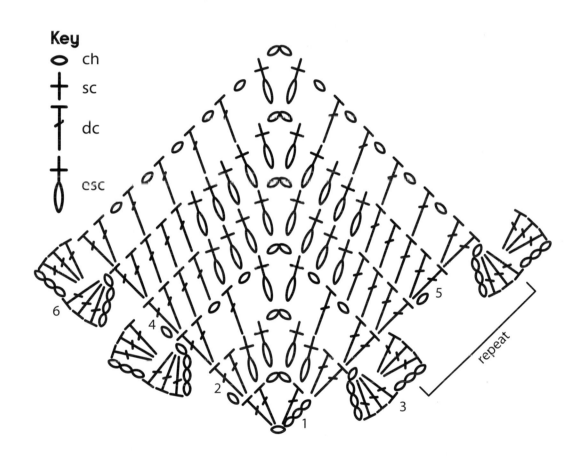

solomon's
wrap

The Solomon's knot stitch is easy when paired with double crochet. Easy, rhythmic stitching will be a breeze in this super lacy, mohair-blend wrap. The edging chases the stitching and is worked simultaneously to complete the project in a snap.

finished size

10½ × 60" (26.5 × 152.5 cm), blocked.

yarn

306 yards (280 m), DK weight (#3 Light).

Shown here: Universal Yarn Amphora (60% acrylic, 20% mohair, 20% alpaca; 306 yds [280 m]/3.5 oz [100g]): #105 Shady Palm, 1 skein.

hook

Size I/9 (5.5 mm).

Adjust hook size if necessary to obtain correct gauge.

notions

2 locking stitch markers (m), yarn needle.

gauge

Blocked: 12 sts = 5" (12.5 cm);
6 rows = 4" (10 cm).

notes

Written instructions and stitch diagrams are provided. Use either type alone, or both together as needed.

Special Stitches

Solomon's Knot (SK)

Pull up a ½" (1.3 cm) lp, yo and pull through the stitch.

Picot

Ch 6, 3-dc-cl (see immediately below) in 5th ch from hook, ch 1.

3 Double Crochet Cluster (3-dc-cl)

[Yo, insert hook in indicated stitch, yo, pull up a lp, yo, pull through 2 lps on hook] 3 times, yo, pull through all 4 lps on hook.

The General Plan

Work from both the inside of the ball and the outside at the same time. One end is used for the edging and the other end for the body of the project until the edging is complete. Work the length. After 4 rows are established, put a marker in the live stitch. Working the same ball of yarn, begin the edging.

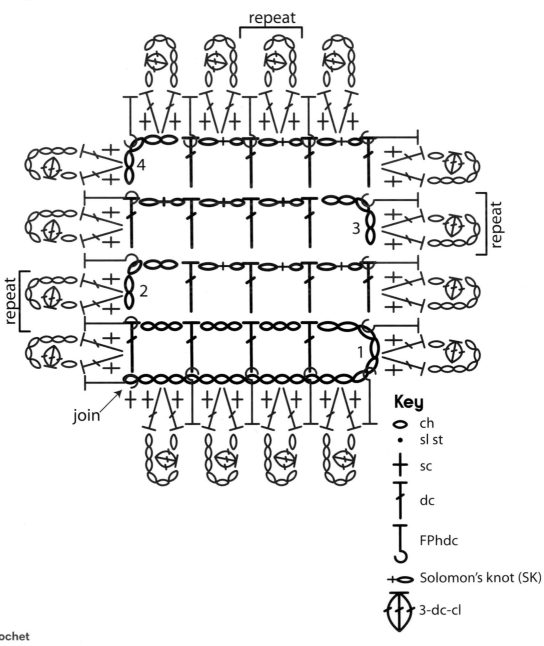

Key

○	ch
•	sl st
+	sc
†	dc
	FPhdc
⊶	Solomon's knot (SK)
	3-dc-cl

Wrap

Pulling from the center of the ball of yarn, ch 205.

Row 1: (RS) Dc in the 9th ch from hook (counts as SK, dc, ch 2), *ch 3, sk 2 chs, dc in next ch; rep from * across.

Row 2: Ch 5, turn, *dc in next dc, SK (see Special Stitches), ch 1**; sk SK and ch-1; rep from * across, ending last rep at **, sk next 2 ch,, dc in 3rd ch of beg ch-5.

Row 3: Ch 5, turn, *dc in next dc, SK, ch 1**, sk 1 SK and ch-1; rep from * across, ending last rep at **, sk next 2 chs, dc in 3rd ch of beg ch-5.

Row 4: Rep Row 3.

After 4 rows are established, place a locking stitch marker in the live stitch and come back to it after beginning edging.

Simultaneous Edging: Working from the same ball of yarn, pulling from the outside of the ball; join new yarn with RS facing, working in underside of foundation Row 1 in end st, sc in end dc, *(sc, dc, picot [see Special Stitches], dc, sc) in next sp (or row-end when working along the short edge), FPhdc around post of next st (or row when working along the short edge); rep from * across. Place locking stitch marker in last edging stitch and resume working body of the wrap.

Rows 5-14: Rep Row 3. Remove the locking stitch marker and resume pattern.

Continue Simultaneous Edging, working along short side of wrap, then long side, then remaining short side; join with sl st in first sc. Fasten off.

Finishing

Weave In all ends.

market
bag

Linked stitches make a more solid fabric than traditional stitches, so they're the perfect foundation for this floral market bag. Worked in the round from the bottom up, the strap continues in the same easy-to-memorize pattern for an interesting, lacy (but strong) shoulder strap.

finished size

13 × 12" (33 × 30.5 cm), strap 23 × 2" (58.5 × 5 cm).

yarn

432 yards (400 m), DK weight (#3 Light).

Shown here: Berroco Remix Light (30% nylon, 27% cotton, 24% acrylic, 10% silk, 9% linen; 432 yd [395 m]/3.5 oz [100g]): #6922 Buttercup, 1 skein.

hook

Size G/6 (4 mm) and H/8 (5 mm).

Adjust hook size if necessary to obtain correct gauge.

notions

Locking stitch marker (m), yarn needle.

gauge

Using larger hook, 21 sts and 11 rows = 4" (10 cm) in pattern.

notes

This bag is worked from the bottom up.

Written instructions and stitch diagrams are provided. Use either type alone, or both together as needed.

Special Stitches

3 Double Crochet Cluster (3-dc-cl)

[Yo, insert hook in indicated stitch, yo, pull up a lp, yo, pull through 2 lps on hook] 3 times, yo, pull through all 4 lps on hook.

Body (worked in rounds)

With smaller hook, fdc (see Glossary) 58, do not turn.

Rnd 1: Ch 2 (does not count as a st), 2 linked dc (see Glossary) in the short side of the base, place a marker in the first st, linked dc in the underside of the 58 foundation sts, place 2 linked dc in the short side of the base, linked dc in the next 56 stitches along the opposite long edge of the base, join with sl st in first marked st—120 linked dc.

Rnd 2: Ch 2 (does not count as a st), 2 linked dc in the short side of the base, pm in the first st, linked dc in the underside of the 58 fdcs, place 2 linked dc in the short side of the base, linked dc in the next 58 sts along the opposite long edge of the base; join with sl st in first marked st—120 linked dc.

Rnd 3: Work 120 linked dc (see Glossary) around; join with sl st in first st.

Rnd 4: Change to larger hook. (Begin pattern) Ch 3 (counts as first dc), *sk 3 sts, (3-dc-cl [see Special Stitches], ch 3, sc, ch 3, 3-dc-cl) all in next st, sk 3 sts**, dc in next st; rep from * around, ending last rep at **; join with sl st in top beg ch-3.

Rnd 5: Ch 6 (counts as first dc plus 3 chs), *sk next cl, 3-dc-cl in sc, ch 3, sk next cl, dc in next dc, ch 3; rep from * around, ending with sk next cl, 3-dc-cl in sc, ch 3, sk next cl; join with sl st in 3rd ch of beg ch-6.

Rnd 6: Ch 3, *(3-dc-cl, ch 3, sc, ch 3, 3-dc-cl) all in next cl**, dc in next dc; rep from * around, ending last rep at **; join with sl st in top of beg ch-3.

Rnds 7-30: Rep Rnds 5 and 6.

Do not fasten off.

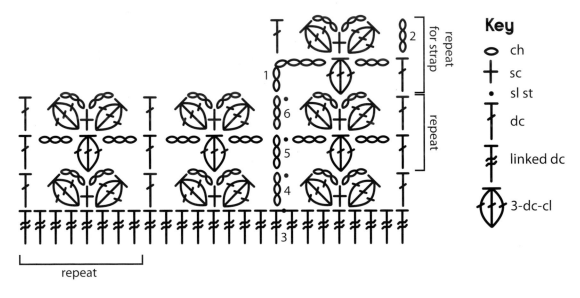

Key

○	ch
†	sc
•	sl st
╪	dc
╪	linked dc
⬙	3-dc-cl

Begin Strap

Note: The strap is worked in turned rows over 1 pattern repeat.

Row 1: Ch 6 (counts as first dc plus 3 chs), turn, sk next cl, 3-dc-cl in sc, ch 3, sk next cl, dc in last st.

Row 2: Ch 3 (counts as first dc), turn, (3-dc-cl, ch 3, sc, ch 3, 3-dc-cl) all in cl, dc in last st.

Rows 3-36: Rep Rows 1 and 2.

Row 37: Rep Row 1.

Cut yarn, leaving a 6" (15 cm) tail.

With yarn tail and yarn needle, sew bag strap opposite the origin of the strap.

Strap Edging

Join new yarn at base where strap is connected to bag with (sc, ch 1, sc) in each ch-3 side turning chain space along the strap edge, sc on bag body (it doesn't matter where). Fasten off.

Repeat for opposite long edge of strap.

Finishing

Weave in ends.

one motif baby
blanket

Worked from the center outward, this one large motif grows on every round. Enjoy each ripple and round as the pattern blossoms before your eyes! It's a generous size for baby and will make an excellent lap blanket or play mat as the tot grows.

finished size

16 × 25" (40.5 × 63.5 cm).

yarn

867 yards (792 m), worsted weight (#4 Medium).

Shown here: Red Heart Comfort (100% acrylic; 867 yd [792 m]/16 oz [454g]): #3231 Vintage Purple, 1 skein.

hook

Size J/10 (6 mm).

Adjust hook size if necessary to obtain correct gauge.

notions

Locking stitch markers (m), yarn needle.

gauge

Rnds 1–4 = 4¼" (11 cm).

notes

All rounds are worked on the right side without turning.

Written instructions and stitch diagrams are provided. Use either type alone, or both together as needed.

Special Stitches

Beginning 3 Double Crochet Cluster (beg 3-dc-cl)

Ch 3, yo, insert hook in indicated stitch, yo and pull up lp, yo, draw through 2 lps on hook, yo, insert hook in same stitch, yo and pull up lp, yo, draw through 2 lps on hook, draw through all 3 lps on hook.

3 Double Crochet Cluster (3-dc-cl)

[Yo, insert hook in indicated stitch, yo, pull up a lp, yo, pull through 2 lps on hook] 3 times, yo, pull through all 4 lps on hook.

V-stitch (V-st)

(Dc, ch 2, dc) in same st or sp.

Stitch Abbreviations

4-tr-tog (4 trebles [see Glossary] together)

5-tr-tog (5 trebles together)

dc2tog (double crochet 2 together)

The General Plan

Work from the middle outward until you run out of yarn.

Blanket

Ch 4; join with sl st to form a ring.

Rnd 1: (RS) Working in ring, beg 3-dc-cl (see Special Stitches) in ring, [ch 3, 3-dc-cl (see Special Stitches)] 5 times in ring, ch 1; join with hdc in beg cl (counts as a ch 3 throughout)—6 cl, 6 ch-3 sps.

Rnd 2: Beg 3-dc-cl in first ch-3 sp (half corner made), *ch 3, (3-dc-cl, ch 3, 3-dc-cl) in next ch-3 sp; rep from * around, ending with 3-dc-cl in first ch-3 sp, ch 1; join with hdc in beg 3-dc-cl—12 3-dc-cl.

Rnd 3: Ch 1, sc in first ch-3 sp, *ch 5, sc in next ch-3 sp; rep from * around, ch 2; join with dc in first sc (counts as a ch 5 throughout)—12 ch-5 sps, 12 sc.

Rnd 4: Ch 1, sc in first ch-5 sp, *ch 5, sc in next ch-5 sp; rep from * around, ch 2; dc in first sc to join—12 ch-5 sps, 12 sc.

Rnd 5: *Ch 1, 5 dc in next sc, ch 1, sc in next ch-5 sp; rep from * around, ending with last sc in the dc-join of previous round; join with sl st in top of first dc.

Rnd 6: Ch 3, 4-tr-tog over next 4 dc (counts as beg 5-tr-tog), ch 7, *5-tr-tog over next 5 dc, ch 7; rep from * around; join with sl st in top beg 5-tr-tog—12 5-tr-tog, 12 ch-7 sps.

Rnd 7: (Beg 3-dc-cl, ch 3, 3-dc-cl, ch 3, 3-dc-cl) in beg 5-tr-tog, *ch 3, sc in next ch-7 sp, ch 3, (3-dc-cl, ch 3, 3-dc-cl, ch 3, 3-dc-cl) in next 5-tr-tog; rep from * around, ch 3, sc in next ch-7 sp, ch 3; join with sl st in beg 3-dc-cl—12 groups.

Rnd 8: Sl st over to center 3-dc-cl of first 3-cl group, ch 1, (sc, ch 5, sc) in same st, *ch 5, sc in next sc, ch 5**, (sc, ch 5, sc) in center 3-dc-cl; rep from * around, ending last rep at **; join with sl st in first sc—36 ch-5 sps.

Rnd 9: Sl st in first ch-5 sp, ch 4 (counts as first tr throughout), (3 tr, ch 3, 4 tr) in same sp, *V-st (see Special Stitches) in next sc**, (4 tr, ch 3, 4 tr) in next ch-5 sp; rep from * around, ending last rep at **; join with sl st in top of beg ch-4—96 tr, 12 V-sts, 12 ch-3 sps.

Rnd 10: Sl st in each of next 3 tr and in next ch-3 sp, ch 1, (sc, ch 5, sc) in same sp, *ch 6, sk next 4 tr, dc2tog over 2 dc of next V-st, ch 6**, sk next 4 tr, (sc, ch 5, sc) in next ch-3 sp; rep from * around, ending last rep at **; join with sl st in first sc—24 ch-6 sps, 12 ch-5 sps.

Note: Rnd 11 will turn this 12-pointed piece into a square. If it helps, place locking stitch markers in the first, 4th, 7th, and 10th ch-5 sps to indicate the 4 corners of the square.

Rnd 11: Sl st in first marked ch-5 sp, ch 4, (4 tr, ch 3, 5 tr) in same ch-5 sp, *[ch 4, sk next ch-6 sp, V-st in next dc2tog, ch 4, sk next ch-6 sp, (3 sc, ch 3, 3 sc) in next ch-5 sp] twice, ch 4, sk next ch-6 sp, V-st in next dc2tog, ch 4, sk next ch-6 sp**, (5 tr, ch 3, 5 tr) in marked corner ch-4 sp; rep from * twice; rep from * around, ending last rep at **; join with sl st in top beg ch-4—40 tr, 12 V-sts, 48 sc.

Key

o	ch		
•	sl st	⌇	tr
+	sc		
T	hdc	⬙	beg 3-dc-cl
┬	dc	⬥	3-dc-cl

Rnd 12: Sl st in next 4 tr and in next ch-4 sp, (beg 3-dc-cl, ch 3, 3-dc-cl, ch 3, 3-dc-cl, ch 3, 3-dc-cl) in same ch-4 sp, ch 5, *[(3-dc-cl, ch 3, 3-dc-cl) in next V-st, ch 5, sk next ch-4 sp, (sc, ch 3, sc) in next ch-3 sp, ch 5, sk next ch-4 sp] twice, (3-dc-cl, ch 3, 3-dc-cl) in next V-st, ch 5, sk next ch-4 sp**, (3-dc-cl, ch 3, 3-dc-cl, ch 3, 3-dc-cl, ch 3, 3-dc-cl) in next corner ch-3 sp; rep from * around, ending last rep at **; join with sl st in first cl—40 cl.

Rnd 13: Sl st in first ch-3 sp, (beg 3-dc-cl, ch 3, 3-dc-cl) in same sp, [ch 3, (3-dc-cl, ch 3, 3-dc cl) in next ch-3 sp] twice, *[ch 5, sk next ch-5 sp, 3 dc in next ch-3 sp, ch 5, sk next ch-5 sp, 3 sc in next ch-3 sp] twice, ch 5, sk next ch-5 sp, 3 dc in next ch-3 sp, ch 5, sk next ch-5 sp**, 3-dc-cl, ch 3, 3-dc cl) in next ch-3 sp, [ch 3, (3-dc-cl, ch 3, 3-dc cl) in next ch-3 sp] twice; rep from * around, ending last rep at **; join with sl st in first cl—18 cl, 36 dc, 24 sc.

Rnd 14: Sl st in next ch-3 sp, ch 3 (counts as dc here and throughout), dc in same ch-3 sp, *sk next cl, 2 dc in next ch-3 sp, sk next cl, (2 dc, ch 3, 2 dc) in corner ch-3 sp, sk next cl, 2 dc in next ch-3 sp, sk next cl, 2 dc in next ch-3 sp, sk next cl, [4 dc in next ch-5 sp, dc in next 3 dc, 4 dc in next ch-5 sp, dc in blo only of next 3 sc] twice, 4 dc in next ch-5 sp, dc in next 3 dc, 4 dc in next ch-5 sp**, sk next cl, 2 dc in next ch-3 sp; rep from * around, ending last rep at **; join with sl st in top of beg ch-3—51 dc per side.

Rnd 15: Ch 3, dc in each dc around working (2 dc, ch 3, 2 dc) in each ch-3 corner sp—55 dc per side.

Rnd 16: Rep Rnd 15—59 dc per side.

Rnd 17: Ch 2 (does not count as a st), sk first st, [BPdc around the post of next dc, FPdc around the post of next dc] 4 times, BPdc around the post of next dc, *(dc, ch 3, dc) in next corner ch-3 sp, [BPdc around the post of next dc, FPdc around the post of next dc] 29 times, BPdc around the post of next dc; rep from * twice, [BPdc around the post of next dc, FPdc around the post of next dc] 24 times, BPdc around the post of next dc, FPdc around the post of next beg ch-3 in previous round; join with sl st in first BPdc—61 sts on each side.

Rnd 18: Ch 2 (does not count as a st), sk first st, [BPdc around the post of next st, FPdc around the post of next st] 5 times, *(dc, ch 3, dc) in next corner ch-3 sp, [FPdc around the post of next st, BPdc around the post of next st] 30 times, FPdc around the post of next st; rep from * twice, [FPdc around the post of next st, BPdc around the post of next st] 25 times, FPdc around the post of last st; join with sl st in first BPdc—63 sts on each side. Fasten off.

Rnd 19: With RS facing, join yarn with sc in any corner ch-3 sp, (ch 3, sc) in same corner ch-3 sp, *[ch 3, sk next 3 sts, sc in next st] across to last 3 sts before corner, ch 3, sk next 3 sts**, (sc, ch 3, sc) in corner ch-3 sp; rep from * around, ending last rep at **; join with sl st in first sc—16 ch-3 sps across each side and 4 ch-3 corner sps.

Rnd 20: Sl st in first ch-3 sp, (beg 3-dc-cl, ch 3, 3-dc-cl) in same corner ch-3 sp, ch 3, (3-dc-cl, ch 3) in each ch-3 sp across to next corner**, (3-dc-cl, ch 3, 3-dc-cl) in corner ch-3 sp; rep from * around, ending last rep at **; join with sl st in beg 3-dc-cl—18 cl per side and 4 ch-3 corner sps.

Rnd 21: Sl st in first ch-3 corner sp, ch 1, (sc, ch 3, sc) in same corner ch-3 sp, ch 3, (sc, ch 3) in each ch-3 sp across to next corner ch-3 sp**, (sc, ch 3, sc) in next corner ch-3 sp; rep from * around, ending last rep at **; join with sl st in first sc—18 ch-3 sps per side and 4 ch-3 corner sps.

Rnds 22 and 23: Rep Rnds 20 and 21.

Rnd 24: Rep Rnd 20—22 cl per side and 4 ch-3 corner sps.

Rnd 25: Sl st in first ch-3 corner sp, ch 6 (counts as first dc, ch 3), dc in same corner ch-3 sp, *dc in next cl, [3 dc in next ch-3 sp, dc in next cl] across to next corner**, (dc, ch 3, dc) in corner ch-3 sp; rep from * around, ending last rep at **; join with sl st in 3rd ch of beg ch-6—87 dc per side and 4 ch-3 corner sps.

Rnd 26: Ch 3, dc in each dc around, working (dc, ch 3, dc) in each ch-3 corner sp; join with sl st in first dc—89 dc per side.

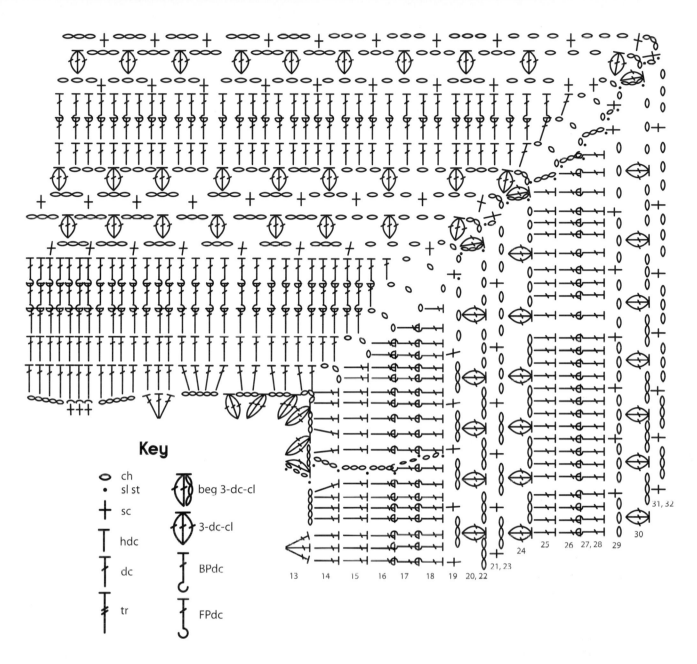

Key

- ⬭ ch
- • sl st
- ✚ sc
- ⊤ hdc
- ⊦ dc
- ⊦ tr
- ⬯ beg 3-dc-cl
- ⬯ 3-dc-cl
- ⊦ BPdc
- ⊦ FPdc

Rnd 27: Sl st in first ch-3 corner sp, ch 6, dc in same corner ch-3 sp, [FPdc around next st, BPdc around next st] across to last st before next corner, FPdc around last st**, (dc, ch 3, dc) in next corner ch-3 sp; rep from * around, ending last rep at **; join with sl st in first dc—91 sts per side and 4 ch-3 corner sps.

Rnd 28: Rep Rnd 27—93 sts per side and 4 corner sps.

Rnd 29: Sl st in first ch-3 corner sp, ch 1, (sc, ch 3, sc) in same corner ch-3 sp, sc in next st, *[ch 3, sk next 2 sts, sc in next st] across to last 3 sts before corner, ch 3, sk next 2 sts, sc in next st**, (sc, ch 3, sc) in corner ch-3 sp; rep from * around, ending last rep at **; join with sl st in first sc—23 ch-3 sps per side and 4 ch-3 corner sps.

Rnd 30: Rep Rnd 20—25 cl per side and 4 ch-3 corner sps.

Rnds 31 and 32: Rep Rnd 21. Fasten off at end of last rnd.

Finishing

Weave in ends.

Stitch Key

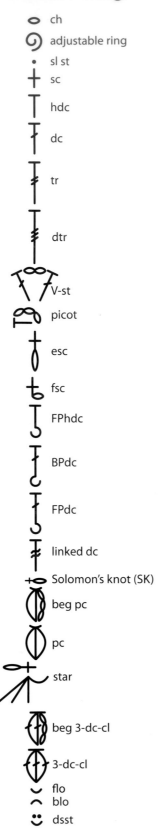

- ch
- adjustable ring
- sl st
- sc
- hdc
- dc
- tr
- dtr
- V-st
- picot
- esc
- fsc
- FPhdc
- BPdc
- FPdc
- linked dc
- Solomon's knot (SK)
- beg pc
- pc
- star
- beg 3-dc-cl
- 3-dc-cl
- flo
- blo
- dsst

Abbreviations

3-dc-cl 3 double crochet cluster

4-tr-tog 4 trebles together

5-tr-tog 5 trebles together

beg pc beginning popcorn

beg 3-dc-cl beginning 3 double crochet cluster

blo back loop only

BP back post

BPdc back post double crochet

ch chain

cl cluster

dc double crochet

dc blo double crochet in back loop only

dec decrease

dc2tog double crochet two together

dsst double slip stitch

dtr double treble crochet

esc extended single crochet

fdc foundation double crochet

fhdc foundation half double crochet

flo front loop only

FP front post

FPdc front post double crochet

FPhdc front post half double crochet

fsc foundation single crochet

hdc half double crochet

lp(s) loop(s)

pc popcorn

pm place marker

rep repeat

RS right side

sc single crochet

sc2tog single crochet two stitches together

sk skip

SK Solomon's knot

sl slip

sl st slip stitch

sp(s) space(s)

st(s) stitch(es)

tr treble crochet

WS wrong side

yd yard

yo yarn over

Glossary

Making an Adjustable Ring

Make a large loop with the yarn (**figure 1**). Holding the loop with your fingers, insert hook in loop and pull working yarn through loop (**figure 2**). Yarn over hook, pull through loop on hook. Continue to work indicated number of stitches in loop (**figure 3**; shown in single crochet). Pull on yarn tail to close loop (**figure 4**).

figure 1   figure 2

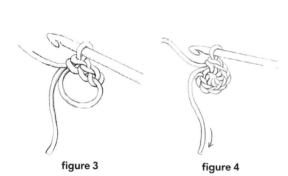

figure 3   figure 4

Chain (ch)

Make a slipknot on hook, *yarn over and draw through loop of slipknot; repeat from * drawing yarn through last loop formed.

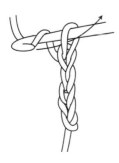

Single Crochet (sc)

*Insert hook in stitch, yarn over and pull up loop (**figure 1**), yarn over and draw through both loops on hook (**figure 2**); repeat from *.

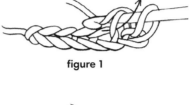

figure 1

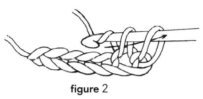

figure 2

Slip Stitch (sl st)

*Insert hook in stitch, yarn over and draw loop through stitch and loop on hook; repeat from *.

Half Double Crochet (hdc)

*Yarn over, insert hook in stitch, yarn over and pull a loop through stitch (three loops on hook), yarn over (**figure 1**) and draw through all the loops on the hook (**figure 2**); repeat from *.

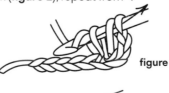

figure 1

figure 2

Foundation Double Crochet (fdc)

Chain 3. Yarn over, insert hook in 3rd chain from hook, yarn over and pull up loop (3 loops on hook) (**figure 1**), yarn over and draw through 1 loop (1 chain made—shaded) (**figure 2**), (yarn over and draw through 2 loops—**figure 3**) 2 times—1 foundation double crochet with chain at bottom (**figure 4**). *Yarn over, insert hook under the 2 loops of the chain at the bottom of the stitch just made, yarn over and pull up loop (3 loops on hook) (**figure 5**), yarn over and draw through 1 loop (1 chain made), (yarn over and draw through 2 loops) 2 times (**figure 6**). Repeat from *.

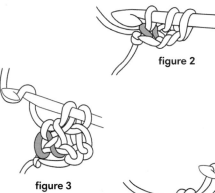

figure 1

figure 2

figure 3

figure 4

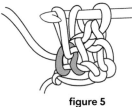

figure 5

figure 6

Double Crochet (dc)

*Yarn over, insert hook in stitch, yarn over and pull up loop (3 loops on hook; **figure 1**), yarn over and draw through 2 loops (**figure 2**), yarn over and draw through remaining 2 loops (**figure 3**); repeat from *.

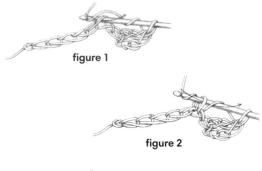

figure 1

figure 2

figure 3

Treble Crochet (tr)

*Yarn over hook twice, insert hook into next indicated stitch, yarn over hook and draw up a loop (4 loops on hook; **figure 1**), yarn over hook and draw it through 2 loops (**figure 2**), yarn over hook and draw it through the next 2 loops, yarn over hook and draw it through remaining 2 loops on hook (**figure 3**), repeat from *

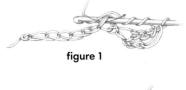

figure 1

figure 2

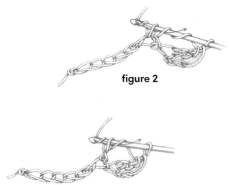

figure 3

Reverse Single Crochet (rev sc)

Working from left to right, insert crochet hook into a knit edge stitch, draw up a loop, bring yarn over hook, and draw this loop through the first one. *Insert hook into next stitch to right (**figure 1**), draw up a loop, bring yarn over hook again (**figure 2**), and draw this loop through both loops on hook (**figure 3**); repeat from *.

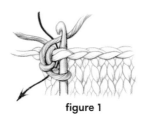

figure 1

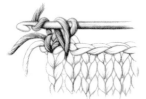

figure 2

figure 3

Front Post Double Crochet (FPdc)

Yarn over, insert hook from front to back to front around post of indicated stitch, yarn over and pull up loop, [yarn over, draw through 2 loops on hook] 2 times.

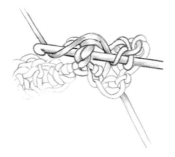

Back Post Double Crochet (BPdc)

Yarn over, insert hook from back to front to back around post of stitch to be worked, yarn over and pull up loop, [yarn over, draw through 2 loops on hook] 2 times.

Single Crochet Two Together (sc2tog)

Insert hook in indicated stitch or space, yarn over and pull up loop (2 loops on hook, **figure 1**), insert hook in next stitch or space, yarn over and pull up loop (3 loops on hook), yarn over and draw through all 3 loops on hook (**figure 2**)—1 stitch decreased (**figure 3**).

figure 1

figure 2

figure 3

Double Crochet Two Together (dc2tog)

Yarn over, insert hook in indicated stitch or space, yarn over (**figure 1**) and pull up loop, yarn over (**figure 2**), [draw through 2 loops] 2 times (3 loops on hook), yarn over (**figure 3**), draw through all loops on hook—1 stitch decreased (**figure 4**).

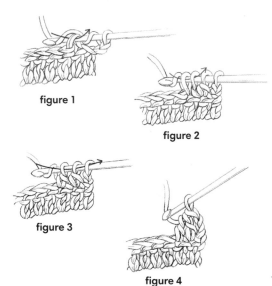

figure 1

figure 2

figure 3

figure 4

Linked Double Crochet (ldc)

First st: Ch 3, insert the hook in the 2nd ch from hook, yo and draw through (two loops now on hook), insert hook in next st (**figure 1**), yo and draw up a loop, [yo and pull through 2 loops on the hook] twice (**figure 2**).

Next and subsequent stitches: Insert the hook into the horizontal bar of the first st (**figure 3**), yo and draw up a loop, insert hook in next stitch on the row, [yo and pull through 2 loops on hook] twice.

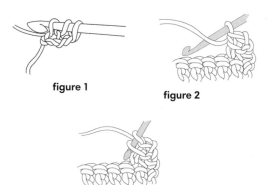

figure 1

figure 2

figure 3

Photo: Peggy McHale Joseph

About the Author

This is the sixth crochet book Ellen Gormley has written—she just can't stop! She began with *Go Crochet! Afghan Design Workbook* in 2011 and continued with *Go Crochet! Skillbuilder, Crocheting Clothes Kids Love* (with Shelby Allaho), *Learn Bruges Lace,* and *Marvelous Crochet Motifs.* Ellen enjoyed five seasons as a crochet expert and cast member of the TV show *Knit and Crochet Now!* Ellen also served as editor of *Crochet!* magazine for three years. She's now on YouTube as she interacts with crocheters and knitters worldwide with live posts, giveaways, tutorials, swatching experiences, and more.

Ellen's place in the crochet world is secure. She has designed and published more than 400 designs over 14 years in countless magazines and books, and she receives accolades for her clear and effective teaching and approachable, fun energy as a spokesperson. Ellen has been known to travel with crocheters to distant places in search of fun and yarn. (Check her website, EllenGormley.com, for upcoming trips.) And if you need to ask questions or see helpful tutorials, visit her YouTube channel at www.youtube.com/EllenGormley.

Ellen is a marathon runner and a cake enthusiast. She lives near Cincinnati, Ohio, with her husband, Tom, and their wildly smart, interesting, and fun teenagers, Maura and Patrick.

Acknowledgments

Thank you to the yarn companies who generously supplied yarn for this book! You provide exciting, interesting, and inspiring products.

Thank you to my crochet support team: Haley Zimmerman, Brenda Bourg, Rebecca Velasquez, Marly Bird, Susie Allen, and Sara Meyer.

Thank you to my BRF, Lisa.

I'd like to acknowledge my YouTube Subscribers, who share my excitement for crochet.

Most importantly, I'd like to acknowledge that there's no creativity or inspiration without God, and I'm supremely grateful for those gifts.

Metric Conversion Chart

To Convert	To	Multiply By
Inches	Centimeters	2.54
Centimeters	Inches	0.4
Feet	Centimeters	30.5
Centimeters	Feet	0.03
Yards	Meters	0.9
Meters	Yards	1.1

Yarn Sources

Anzula
anzula.com

Berroco
berroco.com

Cascade Yarns
cascadeyarns.com

Lion Brand
lionbrand.com

Manos del Uruguay
manosyarns.com

Patons
knitpatons.com

Quince & Co.
quinceandco.com

Red Heart
redheart.com

Skacel
skacelknitting.com

Universal Yarn
universalyarn.com

Find more ways to stitch your way through your stash!

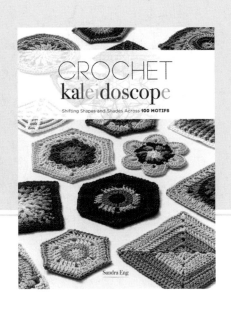
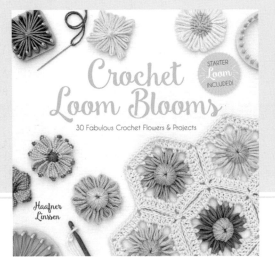
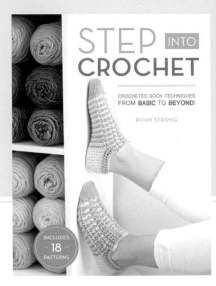